Praise for *Body Respect*

"It is profoundly important to address the shortcomings in health discourse, particularly when misinformation is harming the population. *Body Respect* is a ground-breaking, dogma-busting book that will change how you think about health forever."

> —*Christopher Kennedy Lawford, New York Times bestselling author and former UN Goodwill Ambassador for Drug Treatment and Care*

"Linda and Lucy have written the rare self-help book that places the personal decisions about how to care for ourselves in the larger context of the world's unequal opportunities, judgment, and bias. Acknowledging these injustices and honoring our diverse experiences in our diverse bodies, we each still face the question of what we will do today to be good to ourselves. *Body Respect* gives us a way to think about our decisions—especially the challenge of valuing ourselves in an indifferent or hostile world—and the concrete steps to feeling better in our bodies right now."

> —*Deb Burgard, PhD, psychologist, eating disorders specialist, and HAES pioneer*

"In a world where positive, uplifting, and scientifically grounded messages about weight are sorely lacking—Linda Bacon and Lucy Aphramor have given us a bright light of hope. *Body Respect* is a must-read book for anyone interested in the complex and timely topic of weight. The authors provide information about food, science, psychology, and more that cuts right to the core of why we're so confused around body fat. This breakthrough book is written with both compassion for the human heart and a sharp eye for what the research is really saying. It's practical, information rich, easy to read, and yet profound in its outlook. *Body Respect* lives up to its title—it offers deep respect for those of us who are tired of the same old messages about weight and body fat that fail to honor the fullness of our humanity. It's time for a new approach to weight. Linda Bacon and Lucy Aphramor have given us just that. Bravo."

> —*Marc David, MA, author and founder of the Institute for the Psychology of Eating*

"Drs. Bacon and Aphramor have created a smart, engaging, and compassionate guide that exposes why the 'eat less, exercise more' weight loss mantra fails so miserably, and how to achieve true health and wellness. From the frustrated dieter to the nurse, doctor, and public health official, *Body Respect* is transformative for the individual reader, as well as a wake-up call for the real public health crisis America faces: illness and suffering brought on by chronic stress associated with poverty, social inequality, oppression, and stigma."

—*Katja Rowell MD, author of* Love Me, Feed Me *and childhood feeding specialist, thefeedingdoctor.com*

"*Body Respect* brilliantly explains why guiding ourselves and others toward better health rather than toward weight loss is not only a more effective and compassionate approach to struggles with eating and weight—but one that is solidly rooted in fact and science. This book is a must-read for those who struggle and who suffer from our culture's pervasively negative attitude toward fat . . . and for those who want to help them."

—*Anita Johnston, PhD, author of* Eating in the Light of the Moon

"With *Body Respect* Linda Bacon and Lucy Aphramor build on their impressive contributions to *Health at Every Size*. Whether you're a seasoned activist or new to the scene, this book will prove an invaluable addition to the literature debunking fat-phobic health discourse. *Body Respect* is an essential tool for those seeking well-being without stigma."

—*Charlotte Cooper, PhD, psychotherapist*

"These intrepid authors outline the most significant indicators of health and issue a clarion call to reassert our attention to aspects of people's health we can influence apart from body weight. For those who dare to pick up this book and engage with the evidence that is so clearly presented, the power to transform an entire body paradigm is in your hands."

—*Jacqui Gingras, PhD, RD, cofounder of Critical Dietetics*

"This is an important book that should be mandatory reading for every health professional. It provides a compelling argument that issues of body weight, in the name of health, should be reframed to focus on healthy behaviors, not a number on a scale. The authors do an excellent job of laying out the flaws in the obesity research, including the 'obesity paradox.' They blow the whistle on the insanity of dieting, which not only is ineffective, but is one of the quickest ways to assure long-term weight gain, while assaulting the mind and body of the individual."

—*Evelyn Tribole, MS, RD, coauthor of* Intuitive Eating

"Weight is a poor proxy for health, and in their extraordinary and thorough book, Bacon and Aphramor bring just the right amounts of science, wisdom, and compassion to map a more peaceful, sustainable, and equitable road to health. This book will help to alleviate the shame and blame experienced by people who worry about their body size and should be read by every student and professional in the many health-related fields of practice."

—*Judith Matz, LCSW, coauthor of* The Diet Survivors
Handbook *and* Beyond a Shadow of a Diet

"Linda Bacon and Lucy Aphramor have made another important contribution to helping individuals, health care professionals, and policy makers move away from the damaging and fruitless focus on body size that characterizes so much of today's health advice. The title says it all. If you want to support optimal well-being, the place to start is with body respect, understanding, and appreciating the body for the marvelous creation that it is, and then focusing on the true factors that impact health for everyone, regardless of size."

—*Marsha Hudnall, MS, RDN, CD, president and
co-owner of Green Mountain at Fox Run*

"*Body Respect* is the most holistic look at weight and weight loss I have ever read. The authors review nutrition science, physiology, social and psychological factors. They conclude that the dangers of weight are overstated, and that intentional weight loss is nearly always a bad idea. They make a strong case for each person respecting and making peace with their own body, rather than trying to fit into social norms that have little to do with health. They urge a Health at Every Size approach, focusing on health and quality of life instead of on weight. After reading *Body Respect*, I am convinced this is the best approach for most people."

—*David Spero, RN, author of* The Art of Getting Well *and* Diabetes: Sugar-Coated Crisis

"This book is the prescription needed for our fat-shaming society. Bodies are not the problem—making people feel ashamed of their bodies *is* the problem. Thank you, Linda and Lucy, for this critically important book."

—*Connie Sobczak, cofounder of The Body Positive and author of* Embody: Learning to Celebrate Your Unique Body (and Quiet That Critical Voice!)

"In their new book, *Body Respect*, Drs. Bacon and Aphramor present an eye-opening exposé on all that is wrong with our current understanding of and approaches to issues of weight and health on both sides of the 'big pond.' As they so eloquently detail, our prejudices toward larger individuals have created cultures in which scientists routinely publish literature that does not support their conclusions, health professionals recommend interventions that do not result in long-term weight loss or health improvement and for many people lead to increased weight and poorer health, and people who do not meet the ever-diminishing standards of body shape and size are routinely pictured as lazy, gluttonous, and not interested in their own health. The solution they propose—*Body Respect*—honoring body diversity, self-acceptance, and self-love accompanied by paying attention to lovingly feeding and moving our bodies is the antidote for our culture's obsession with weight and all of the attendant negative health and social justice consequences. No health or helping professionals should finish their degree programs without having read this book, and everyone who is struggling with our culture's insanity around these issues will likely improve their health just by reading it! Bravo!"

—*Jon Robison, PhD, MS, professor at Michigan State University*

"Anyone interested in health, weight, and wellness will find something of value in Lucy Aphramor and Linda Bacon's new book: *Body Respect*. Whether you are already a proponent of the Health at Every Size approach, on the fence, or convinced it lacks merit, you are doing yourself a disservice not to read this book from cover to cover and add it to your library. The authors manage to combine their separate voices into one as they deliver the latest, most up-to-date research on the efficacy of HAES, the importance of a weight-neutral approach to wellness, and why we need to give up desperate fad diets in the attempt to change our natural body type. Bacon and Aphramor resist the temptation of weighing their points of view down in too much rhetoric or 'preachy' diatribes and opt to share their research and insights in a casual conversational style."

—*Deah Schwartz, PhD, clinician, author, and educator specializing in eating disorders and body image*

"Everybody needs to read this book. In equal parts shocking, comforting, and inspiring, it is essential reading and a ray of hope in a world of body shaming. This is the tool to build the foundations of a health service based in compassion, respect, and better care for both practitioners and their patients."

—*Amy Godfrey, performance artist for* The Biscuit Chronicles

"A compassionate and critical take on improving health while embracing the complexity of all bodies and considering the health impact of living within a stratified society. *Body Respect* combines a much-needed society-level approach to health with practical steps individuals can take. If we truly want to address the 'obesity epidemic,' respect is the way to do it."

—*Michelle Allison, The Fat Nutritionist*

"Linda Bacon and Lucy Aphramor once again poke huge holes in the conventional 'wisdom' around weight, food, and disease. This book is a must-read for health practitioners, chronic dieters, and anyone who wants the real deal on weight and health."

—*Golda Poretsky, founder of Body Love Wellness and author of* Stop Dieting Now: 25 Reasons to Stop, 25 Ways to Heal

"Building on the wonderful book *Health at Every Size, Body Respect* is a vital read for anyone looking for honesty, understanding, and the truth. Linda and Lucy have shared with us not only why it is so important to do our best to move our focus away from our current culture's narrow definition of weight and health. Importantly and additionally, they have given us the information and support to show us how we can move toward the freedom of well-being, compassion, and respect. Congratulations on your great resource."

—*Dr. Rick Kausman, MD, author of* If Not Dieting, Then What?

"This book is a triumph of compassion over judgment, skepticism over confirmation bias, and evidence over 'everybody knows.' While it will surely appeal to anyone who is interested in looking past the headlines and into the real science of weight and health, this book should be required reading for everyone."

—*Ragen Chastain,* Dances with Fat *blogger and author of* Fat: The Owner's Manual

"*Body Respect* empowers us to respect our own body's wisdom and needs, educating us about the real science and actual truth about the connections between weight and health. But more importantly, *Body Respect* challenges the belief that individual attempts to diet and lose weight will improve public health, explaining how the structured inequality of our economic and social system is the real culprit. Once we acknowledge the central causal role of the cumulative stress of chronic poverty, oppression, discrimination, and weight stigma in weight-associated diseases, we will be on the road to a health care system that can systematically deliver both health and care to everyone, regardless of their weight, size, or socioeconomic status—and not a moment too soon."

—*Margo Maine, PhD, FAED, CEDS, founding member of National Eating Disorders Association and Academy for Eating Disorders and author of* Treatment of Eating Disorders: Bridging the Research-Practice Gap

"The Health at Every Size movement is so important to me personally and professionally, that I couldn't help but be deeply inspired by Linda and Lucy's work, yet again. This book advocates for both the individual and cultural change necessary to experience real freedom. It is backed by science, and is relatable, sprinkled with humor, and full of ways to implement changes in your life based on your own body wisdom. It is life-changing."

—*Carmen Cool, MA, LPC, psychotherapist*

"*Body Respect* challenges health care providers to transform the way they address issues of body size and weight with patients. Bacon and Aphramor argue that traditional approaches emphasizing weight loss often undermine patient health outcomes. They provide guidelines for shifting the emphasis from weight to wellness, and a new standard for supporting patients in the self-management of chronic health conditions."

—*Tim Berthold, MA, editor of* Foundations for Community Health Workers

"An intersectional approach to health—recognizing the devastating impact of stigma and oppressions—is the only way out of our unwinnable and unnecessary war on weight. It's also the way for health professionals to genuinely claim the title of caregiver. Without *Body Respect*, efforts toward health will be counterproductive. This book rights a long-standing wrong."

—*Marilyn Wann, author of* Fat!So?

"Linda and Lucy are gifted thought leaders in a new peace movement called Health at Every Size. This amazing book offers a refreshing perspective on weight in a society that likes to think about bodies as machines that can be tightly controlled if we just tried hard enough. If you are tired of the roller-coaster ride of traditional weight management ideology, this book is for you. It is all about trying different, not harder!"

—*Dana Sturtevant, MS, RD, dietitian and cofounder of Be Nourished, LLC, Portland, OR*

"Congratulations to Lucy and Linda for collaborating on their clear and compassionate book: *Body Respect*! They did an outstanding job presenting complex yet intertwined concepts such as social inequities, structural inequality, and Health at Every Size. Along the way the reader is introduced to the importance of integrative listening, the need to acknowledge the personal and professional journeys required for a new model of health, and why it is imperative we address the proverbial 'elephant in the room' regarding myths and bias on weight and health."

—*Lisa Tealer, NAAFA Board Member Emeritus*

"*Body Respect* sets the record straight: A weight-focused approach to health is harmful, not helpful. Mindful eating and respect for ourselves and others is a sustainable approach that we can thrive with!"

—*Michelle May, MD, author of* Eat What You Love, Love What You Eat *and founder of Am I Hungry?*

"*Body Respect* is a valuable resource for anyone who wants to live healthfully and happily in their body—and the medical practitioners who serve them. Beyond the diet mentality and the media depiction of what a 'good' body looks like, *Body Respect* bravely asks readers to tune into their body's wisdom and expert knowing to guide them. This book contains all of the building blocks necessary to build a positive relationship with the skin that you're in."

—*Mara Glatzel, MSW, life coach for Mindful Eating Programs and Training*

"*Body Respect* should be the go-to resource for all health and wellness experts to finally clear up concerns about weight and health, and to learn strategies for motivating change in their clients. An eye-opening, inspiring book."

—*Rebecca Scritchfield, MA, RDN, ACSM, HFS*

"Linda and Lucy have done a superb job of sifting through complex research on weight science, body politics, exercise science, sociology, and eating psychology to create a comprehensive and actionable manual for living in the bodies we are in."

—*Hilary Kinavey, MS, LPC, cofounder of Be Nourished*

"Linda Bacon and Lucy Aphramor are filling a long-existing gap in the health book market with this smart and accessible text. It's a relief to read about the intersections of health and social justice—and an excellent place to start taking care of yourself as an individual rather than a statistic."

—*Marianne Kirby, founder and blogger of* The Rotund
and coauthor of Lessons from the Fatosphere

"*Body Respect* teaches exactly what grown-ups need for their own sanity and well-being, as well as what is essential to help the next generation avoid the harm of weight-focused approaches to acceptability and health. How can kids learn to care for instead of compare their bodies if the adults in their lives are not modeling this? This book should be required reading for everyone."

—*Kathy Kater, LICSW, eating disorder treatment and
prevention specialist and author of* Healthy Bodies:
Teaching Kids What They Need to Know

"*Body Respect* is a truly eye-opening book that challenged my views on health, dieting, and nutrition in the most positive way. I now feel liberated and capable to celebrate my body and make better choices to ensure happiness and great health for the rest of my life."

—*Nicole Best, student*

"Traverses the personal—with compassion at its core—and the socio-political, which asks us to consider how through structural inequality we are suffering not from an 'obesity epidemic,' but an epidemic of Oppression Syndrome. A great guide to all who know the distress and damage caused by weight stigma and diet failure; there's another way."

—*Louisa Harvey, body image activist*

"This book is a wake-up call. It's time to recognize that the stigma associated with certain bodies is a disease that harms people and robs them of their health and happiness. Linda and Lucy are here to cure us of this ailment, and they have science on their side."

— *Lexi Giblin, PhD, CEDS, executive director and cofounder of Opal: Food+Body Wisdom*

BODY RESPECT

What Conventional Health Books Get Wrong, Leave Out, and Just Plain Fail to Understand about Weight

Linda Bacon, PhD
and
Lucy Aphramor, PhD, RD

BenBella Books, Inc.
Dallas, TX

BENBELLA

BenBella Books, Inc.
10440 N. Central Expressway
Suite #800
Dallas, TX 75231
www.benbellabooks.com
Send feedback to feedback@benbellabooks.com

BenBella is a federally registered trademark.

Printed in the United States of America
10   9   8   7

Library of Congress Cataloging-in-Publication Data

Bacon, Linda.
   Body respect : what conventional health books get wrong, leave out, and just plain fail to understand about weight / Linda Bacon, PhD and Lucy Aphramor, PhD, RD.
      pages cm
   Includes bibliographical references and index.
   ISBN 978-1-940363-19-6 (paperback) — ISBN 978-1-940363-43-1 (electronic)   1.   Weight loss.   2.   Body weight—Regulation.   3.   Self-care, Health.   I. Aphramor, Lucy, 1967–   II. Title.
   RM222.2.B332 2014
   613.2'5—dc23

2014009684

Copyediting by James Fraleigh
Proofreading by Jennifer Greenstein and Lisa Story
Indexing by Jigsaw Indexing
Cover design by Allison Bard
Text design and composition by Publishers' Design and Production Services, Inc.
Printed by Versa Press

Distributed to the trade by Two Rivers Distribution, an Ingram brand
www.tworiversdistribution.com

Special discounts for bulk sales are available. Please contact bulkorders@benbellabooks.com.

CONTENTS

INTRODUCTION

I f you're familiar with Linda's groundbreaking book, *Health at Every Size*, you know that the Health at Every Size® (HAES) movement is all about respect.* It teaches how respecting yourself means learning to treat yourself with kindness, and leads to trusting your body's signals so you follow your appetite instead of a calorie chart. And if you've tried this for yourself, you've discovered how this gentle approach to nutrition and self-care can seriously improve your well-being, whatever your shape or size.

In the science of nutrition, weight, and disease, HAES-based studies find encouraging evidence that we need not fear food—or fat—as agents of illness and despair. These studies also identify paths toward health that avoid dreaded diets and dieting—those rocky shoals against which so many good health intentions have shipwrecked. HAES principles lead to obvious, inexpensive interventions, available both to individuals and health care practitioners, that can produce better health for anyone, no slimming down or body hatred required. Food restriction and fat are off the hook as far as well-being is concerned—thus

---

*Health at Every Size is a registered trademark of the Association of Size Diversity and Health and is used with permission.

moving fat stigma and lack of respect on other grounds into the shameful limelight.

HAES is an entirely hopeful, helpful doctrine. And it belongs not to a single author or set of authors, but to a large and growing cohort of people, lay and professional, who are bound by their mutual desire for respect and equality and by their challenge of commonly held assumptions about fat.

Since *Health at Every Size* came out, there have been new scientific developments and the HAES movement has evolved, so the two of us, Linda Bacon and Lucy Aphramor—both scientists with PhDs—have teamed up to take a fresh look at the ideas and facts behind HAES, including the latest science on diet, weight, and health. In *Body Respect*, we provide you with data that back up the HAES claim that you can find peace and gain better health in *your* body. For health care practitioners, we also raise critical awareness about how to reduce health inequalities, and present new strategies for applying HAES principles more fully to help you support others on that journey. Using peer-reviewed evidence, common sense, and a solid grounding in nutrition science that integrates data from critical public health sources, we debunk obesity myths and guide you through the process of supporting individuals in carving their own paths, knowing that their worth is not in their weight.

Who This Book Is For

First, this book is written for a diverse readership. If you're directly affected by our culture's and the medical community's attitude toward weight and feel uncomfortable in your skin— whatever your size—this book is for you. We don't pretend that it's simply a matter of pulling your socks up and improving your self-image; we do consider the reality of ambivalence and conflicted feelings around size acceptance.

Second, the book is also for medical practitioners and students of health and health care so you, too, can understand the reality of what it's like for someone both society and your medical community regard as "overweight" or "obese"—we actually prefer the term "fat," and we'll explain why later in the book—and for others who live in fear of becoming fat. *Body Respect* helps you understand the damaging ramifications that the "thin is better" mind-set has on people of all sizes and on health inequalities. It makes a persuasive case for a new approach that helps you champion patient dignity and high-quality science. We teach you how to advise people of any size with compassion and body-honoring prescriptions that will guide them toward better health, not toward a certain weight, which will in turn make your job more rewarding. As a guide, at the end of the book you will read about a health care provider, "Billie," and her patient, "Janet," and the challenges they face in managing Janet's diabetes. Billie's experience, which compares conventional practice with an HAES-based approach, illustrates the positive, transformative promise of HAES when adopted by the medical community.

Third, we want to reach out to policy makers and change agents, people on the front lines of community development and their allies in public health working to reduce health inequalities. Where social differences in access to nutritious foods and the personal circumstances needed to be regularly active have been made all too starkly obvious, it is easier to keep our focus on improving individuals' ability to adopt more healthful lifestyle habits. Undoubtedly, eating and exercising affect well-being, and not everyone has access to the material means to be active and eat well, so this social inequity needs to be addressed. But these inequities need attention because they are a travesty; challenging inequity is its own justification and should not require a health improvement checklist to legitimate action. That said, lifestyle doesn't have nearly as much impact on anyone's health as the anti-obesity brigade would have us believe. In fact, the nonmaterial or social effects of living with deprivation and discrimination account for a huge portion of the social gradient in health—much more than that attributed to health behaviors. Yes, everyone needs access to a standard of living that includes good food and the chance to move. But maintaining the primacy of the individual-lifestyle focus—without being transparent about larger influences—is an affront to people living in disadvantage, as it reduces their ill health to poor "choices" and blames them, all the while contributing to the stigma and judgmental thinking that fuels their oppression, worsens their health, and expands the health divide between the advantaged and disadvantaged.

We're vocal about size equality as an issue of social justice. It matters that larger people get judged poorly because of their weight, while thinner people are awarded advantages for their size, and these forms of oppression and privilege need to be challenged. We're against dieting not only because it compromises health (and has actually been proven to cause weight *gain* in the long term) but also because it feeds weight stigma. We don't tell people being fat gives you a heart attack, just like we wouldn't tell someone with yellow teeth that the color of their teeth is going to give them lung cancer. We do ask why the social factors that impact nutrition-sensitive diseases like hypertension and diabetes aren't more widely publicized. In short, we look at what's really behind illness and health, and the truth might surprise you. (Hint: It's not fatness.)

> Lifestyle doesn't have nearly as much impact on anyone's health as the anti-obesity brigade would have us believe.

We could add that the book is also for a fourth audience, the skeptics. But we imagine that camp has members in all of the other three groups. For those who are having a hard time believing that fat is not the problem, stay with us. We know that you may find this book challenging, even aggravating. Already, we realize, your natural skepticism may be rising to the fore. *We all know many people are overweight*, you may be insisting, *that there's an obesity crisis underway. How can these authors just give up on getting people to lose weight for their own sake?* Or even, *How can I, knowing what I know about obesity, in good conscience consider setting all that aside and let people "feel better" about being fat? If they stop caring, won't their weight and poor eating habits spiral even further out of control?*

We ask you to hold those thoughts. Jot your frustrations in the margin, if you must, or dictate an angry memo into your smartphone, but then please read on, because one of the discoveries available to students of HAES—if still unrecognized by too many in the medical and health policy arenas—is that what we think we know about fatness isn't based on actual fact. Alarmingly, neither is what we think we know about lifestyle and health. That's why we wrote this book.

If you've read the first book and are keen to pass the message on, this lighter volume can galvanize the HAES conversation with friends and colleagues. We all need the support of others, and receiving encouragement begins with others understanding why we believe what we believe. In addition to providing the updated science on weight in a concise way for newer readers, *Body Respect* expands on the concepts of how stigma and stress impact well-being introduced in *Health at Every Size*.

Our culture perpetuates the anti-fat myths that keep people depressed and at war with their own bodies: a war where little battles might be won in the short term with a diet, but then lost overall because those who turn to dieting can rarely maintain long term the look that is the accepted norm—one that is not necessarily the best weight for them. And they feel worse about themselves for their failure. It also reinforces the message that they—not the size-stigmatizing culture—are the problem. The guilt-ridden menu that society hands each fat person has led to a severe case of indigestion. Let's throw out the bad advice and discuss new truths that will lead to happier, healthier lives in a fairer world. We need your help to spread the word.

What we think we know about fatness isn't based on actual fact.

Our Mission

Our ultimate goal in *Body Respect* is to champion a paradigm shift—from weight to respect. We examine what weight means to our bodies, how our metabolisms work, and the mechanisms involved, including concepts like "fat" and "calories" that carry so much baggage in our society. We also look at exercise; the science of dieting; biases around fat and bodies, and the impact of prejudice and privilege; and a collection of other cultural factors that affect individuals' health. Throughout, we consider how dogma, myths, and prejudices about fatness, presented as the value-laden "obesity," have trumped actual evidence in our society's evolving views of weight and health.

Relying on fact and sound judgment—and with a passion for fairness and equality—we work in every chapter to separate scientific fact from panicked assumption, unraveling the tangle our culture has made of weight and body shape. From the still-evolving science of modern diet and health, we draw practical lessons and recommendations for effective interventions and policies. We also provide personally applicable, self-help style recommendations that could make a difference in your own life as well as the lives of current or future clients and patients.

Support for You

A warning is in order: If you do get past any initial skepticism about HAES, the next possible hazard is the frustration of dealing with everyone around you who hasn't. It can be exhausting to believe in a new paradigm, a completely changed view of familiar matters, and to have to defend or explain it again and again to everyone mired in old ways of thinking. HAES advocates are not above critique, nor is its theory set in stone or its strategies unanimously agreed upon.[1] It's critical that the movement be open to the inevitability of flaws, gaps, and new perspectives, including proactively seeking input from marginalized communities. But to be positioned as an ambassador for any cause can be draining. That's where education and the HAES community come in. There is a large and growing community around HAES and size acceptance, both online and in associations, and at workshops and conventions. And as books and courses on this topic proliferate, workshops emerge, and more clinics adopt HAES ideas, there is hope for more.

In its promise of real, measurable change—albeit change that will never be documented on a scale or with a tape measure—HAES offers a path forward for all who care about respect and health. With this book, we hope to help map the way.

The Book's Organization

We start by examining common assumptions about body weight and health and then look at weight regulation in individuals. In the process we deconstruct generally accepted ideas and replace them with a more scientifically supported understanding, commonly called "Health at Every Size." We then put all the information together to figure out what conclusions can be drawn about the best way to approach self-care (weight, nutritional well-being, activity, and other related issues), and we highlight the pressing need to put social justice center stage in the health conversation.

A Word about Pronouns

We have written this book with three audiences in mind, which means that the authorial voice is not static. We use "you" consistently throughout the book to speak to those readers, fat, thin, or somewhere in between, who feel the personal pain of weight stigma. An aside: For many people this will include internalized stigma and feelings of shame—decades of fat activism, however, have created an alternative.[2] Our belief in the power of compassion drives us, and a respect for equality is a constant at the heart of this book.

This book has two authors. We use "we" most of the time because it represents our combined thoughts. When we need to specify one author over the other, we use the author's name, Linda or Lucy, rather than "I."

SECTION 1
Deconstructing Weight

CHAPTER 1
Facts and Fiction about Fatness

I t is well established that collectively we got fatter during the second half of the twentieth century. "Experts" warn us that our fat is contagious, spreading from person to person in an epidemic on the same scale as terrorism, and that it will reduce life expectancies and even further global warming. These dire warnings have fueled a war against fat. But is this war warranted? Or does it cause more harm than good?

Untangling this issue is our starting point for the first chapter. We'll invite you to consider radical new perspectives and challenge what has become business as usual in the mainstream world of weight science.

Where Do You Get Your Facts?

How do you "know" what you know? This is a question we have to think about a lot because our ideas about weight conflict so strongly with those held by most others.

They conflict with what we regularly read or hear in the media. They conflict with what we learned in school. They conflict with most "expert" advice and government recommendations. They conflict with what most people believe to be common sense.

We understand if you are skeptical at first about what we write. After all, there is no denying that there are a lot of fat people in industrialized countries. And hardly a day goes by where we are not warned about another health problem caused by fat.

And as we challenge our cherished beliefs about weight and health, we imagine the question will naturally arise: Why should we believe you when so many, including those who are well educated and well accepted as authorities, suggest that what we propose is misinformed and dangerous?

As scientists, we are tempted to "prove" to you that what we say is grounded in fact by jumping immediately to well-reasoned academic arguments bolstered by scientific research. You'll get those scientific arguments throughout the book, but we've learned over time that academic arguments are rarely enough to change how people look at things. Misinformation about weight is so embedded in our cultural landscape that we all absorb it and it becomes deeply ingrained in us. These ideas are so strongly and commonly held that most of us don't even recognize them as assumptions. We think they're "fact."

Because people filter all new information through this cultural lens, it becomes difficult to help them understand the fallacy, even when they're exposed to statistics, logical arguments, or examples of the disparities and pain these attitudes cause. It may be particularly difficult for health professionals to consider new ideas seriously because the old beliefs have been so rooted as normal and appropriate by our education; many of us developed our very expertise and identity by buying in to those beliefs. We also may be expected to carry out practices such as mandatory weighing and weight loss counseling as part of an everyday requirement of our job. Given that our education, identity, reputation, and job expectations are shored up by our allegiance to current beliefs, it is hard for us to even notice that these belief systems are unproven assumptions, let alone to seriously question what we routinely do.

We all absorb the world around us. When we are subjected repeatedly to images of fat people as lazy gluttons and of thin people as attractive, desirable, and healthy, to notions that weight is controllable by diet and exercise or that fat causes people to get sick and die early, it should come as no surprise that these ideas become ingrained in our psyches and we come to believe them. We know it's a hard sell for us to suggest otherwise.

So before we continue with the science, we want to appeal to you on the basis of emotion. Everyone reading this book knows the pain of fighting the war on fat. We've seen it in our friends, family, patients, and others we care for. Many of us face our own struggles around body discontent and food fear.

Take some time to reconnect with those feelings right now. Think for a moment about someone you know who struggles with weight. It could be a friend, a relative, a patient. It could be you. Close your eyes and concentrate on the emotions that go with that, the knowledge that "there's something wrong with my body. My body is a sign of failure."

We were a little hesitant to include a guided visualization, particularly so early in the book, as we know that exercises such as this may cause a shutdown, particularly from those who are more biomedically trained. But it's that very academic distance that gets us into trouble. We get so caught up in allegiance to the metabolic pathways and numbers that we lose track of the people at the heart of it all. This is an opportunity to acknowledge the ubiquitous feelings of pain and helplessness around weight concerns—and to consider how this distress might affect our actions.

It is also an opportunity to take your own personal or professional disquiet seriously. Many health professionals' training leads them to follow guidelines that conflict with what they know from their own practice. They rationalize high failure rates as noncompliance and continue to be obedient to the same advice despite daily evidence of their patients' misery. What's needed instead is a coherent framework for practice that integrates different sources of evidence and knowledge, one that takes emotions, suffering, and stigma into account alongside biomedical data.

It's no longer good enough to do the same thing harder and hope that this time we'll get a different outcome. Instead, it's time to get real and face the fact that there's something going wrong with weight management. Read on to find out more about the safe, sane alternative.

We write this book because we are worried and angry about the harm being done by business as usual in the field of weight and health. We ask you to consider our ideas for the sake of social justice and compassion, and then see if the science moves you as well. Even if you believe that being fat is the dire threat it's portrayed as being, all that drama clearly isn't helping anyone to lose weight or get healthy. Meanwhile, the fear of fatness and the stigma that goes with it hurts everyone, fat or thin, and can be especially damaging to kids.

We need to focus on compassion in outcomes, an idea brought home to me (Linda) most memorably by a teenage girl I met while visiting a school in the throes of an obesity prevention campaign. "Every time I walk down the hall," she told me, "I see posters saying they don't want kids to look like me. How can they possibly think that's helpful? Do they really think that making me and other kids feel that there's something wrong with my body is going to help me—or anyone—eat our fruits and veggies? The only result I've seen is that I've been called 'fatso' more this month than ever."

"Every time I walk down the hall," she told me, "I see posters saying they don't want kids to look like me. How can they possibly think that's helpful? Do they really think that making me and other kids feel that there's something wrong with my body is going to help me—or anyone—eat our fruits and veggies?"

These voices must count, too. The prejudice and distress apparent here are as much an outcome of our practice as the evidence from a validated questionnaire study or a randomized controlled dietary intervention. Remember what we said about developing a coherent framework for practice? If the ways we measure the impact of our interventions don't capture their unintended consequences, then we're not building a robust evidence base to draw on. If the discourse that circulates on fatness doesn't include the views of fat people, then we need to challenge this exclusion in the name of justice, as well as to further balanced reporting and transparent science.

So regardless of whether you accept our interpretation of the data at this point, there is still a strong reason to find an ethical alternative to "tackling obesity": The current model is broken.

Even if you think weight loss might help individuals, it's pretty clear that society's anti-fat messages come at a cost. That doesn't mean doing nothing. Even before reading any further, you know that whether the issue is metabolic syndrome, joint pain, or depression, being treated with respect and supported in health behavior change can't hurt, even if it doesn't bring about weight loss.

Reclaiming Language

Generally in discussion of weight the terms "overweight" and "obese" get used, but we've avoided them in this book unless we needed to use them to report research. To determine whether someone fits into these categories, a formula called the body mass index (BMI) is used, which is defined as weight (in kilograms) divided by height (in meters) squared. A BMI less than 25 is considered "normal," between 25 and 30 is considered "overweight," and 30 and above is classified as "obese." For example, if you're 5′6″ and you're 160 pounds, your BMI would be 25.8 (calculated as 72.5748 kg divided by 2.8103 [1.6764 meters tall, squared]).

However, these categories only give information about your weight relative to your height. They are meaningless in determining someone's *health* status. The terms "overweight" and "obese" also miss the mark. Over what weight? There is no precise weight beyond which you will be unhealthy. And the etymology of the word "obesity" mistakenly implies that a large appetite is the cause.

Using these terms medicalizes and pathologizes weighing over a certain amount, which is why in this book and the HAES movement we leave those terms behind and use a more appropriate term: "fat." There is a growing movement that seeks to reclaim fat as a descriptive term, stripped of its pejorative connotations. This change is supported by many fat acceptance activists and the National Association for the Advancement of Fat Acceptance (NAAFA), a "human rights organization dedicated to improving the quality of life for fat people." NAAFA argues, rightfully so, that fatness is a form of body diversity that should be respected, much like diversity based on skin color or sexual preference.

NAAFA argues, rightfully so, that fatness is a form of body diversity that should be respected, much like diversity based on skin color or sexual preference.

If you find yourself flinching at our use of the word "fat," that's your cultural bias surfacing. Would you similarly flinch if someone called you slim, blonde, or brunette, or named your ethnic group? It's not surprising if you are uncomfortable with using the term "fat," because our culture associates it with "bad." It may not be easy to retrain yourself to just see it as a simple descriptor, but we encourage you to consider it as an important step in supporting size diversity, and a fairer world.

If you glance back over what you've read so far, you'll notice we avoided medical terms for weight (overweight, obese, normal) and used a range of other respectful, descriptive terms—among them, higher and lower body weight, thin and fat, and heavier- and lighter-weight people. We've shown you how you can both avoid misunderstanding *and* use respectful terms to talk about body size.

The Obesity Apocalypse

More people than not in many industrialized countries are now medically defined as fat. We're told this is an obesity epidemic, with its connotations of sickness, danger, and proliferation. Fat people—which is most of us—are viewed as unattractive and a burden on society, and those who more closely fit the thin cultural ideal live in fear of crossing that line. Leading authorities tell us our fat is a national threat, on par with terrorism.[1]

Our alarm about "obesity" is akin to apocalyptic thinking. It clouds our judgment, inducing a panic that interferes with our ability to evaluate the data and let it inform our ideas and practice. And it gives us permission to go to war against fat. Because fat is a physical characteristic, this has really become a war against people and bodies. We are all victims in this obesity war—whether we are fat or fear becoming fat. That said, there is very real evidence that fat people as a group are shouldering the brunt of the burden as they are denied equality in the job market, in health care, and in other areas of life, including basic dignity of representation in the media. The thinner person, although he or she may suffer from intense body dissatisfaction and other negative fallout, is more likely to benefit from this size bias due to reduced competition, preferential treatment, and enhanced sense of entitlement—in other words, "thin privilege."

The Obesity Mythology

In 2002, Surgeon General Richard Carmona, the U.S. government's highest health official, described obesity as "the terror within, a threat that is every bit as real to America as the weapons of mass destruction."[2] Six months before that grave pronouncement, terrorists had destroyed the World Trade Center. The country was on high alert and the fear of continued terrorist action was at the forefront of our minds.

> We don't have an epidemic of obesity; our epidemic is one of judgment, bias, and hyperbole.

Carmona was giving voice to—and helping to construct—the collective irrationality that underlies this "obesity epidemic," creating a specter of terrorists not only in our cities and our airports, but in our kitchens: hamburgers and French fries as weapons of mass destruction. We don't have an epidemic of obesity; our epidemic is one of judgment, bias, and hyperbole.

Calling for a war on fat presumes we have clear evidence of its danger. We do not. It also implies we have a proven arsenal for intervention. We do not. We want to encourage you to suspend your preconceptions and reexamine the evidence. When you do, a very different picture emerges, one where it is the machinery of weight stigma that needs dismantling.

> Calling for a war on fat presumes we have clear evidence of its danger. We do not.

Naming the Myths

The machinery of weight stigma comes packaged in myths. These myths are so often repeated that they get accepted as fact, as if there were hard science backing them up. Looking at the following list of myths, it's not surprising that people want to "do something" about fatness. Let's see what happens when that "something" is a closer inspection of the evidence.

1. Fatness leads to decreased longevity.
2. BMI is a valuable and accurate health measure.
3. Fat plays a substantive role in causing disease.
4. Exercise and dietary restriction are effective weight-loss techniques.
5. We have evidence that weight loss improves health.
6. Health is largely determined by health behaviors.
7. Science is value-free.

For most of us, these statements seem like basic truisms. However, much of what we believe to be true about weight is in fact myth, fueled by the power of money and cultural bias. And public health officials, health care professionals, and scientists are complicit (often unintentionally) in supporting and encouraging the lies and silences. The campaign against fat is not supported by sound science and does not promote health.

The misconceptions propagated about the most basic research on weight are astounding. Let's take a look at some of them.

(Note: The following information on obesity myths was simplified and paraphrased from a peer-reviewed article that we coauthored, "Weight Science: Evaluating the Evidence for a Paradigm Shift," which includes citations to the supporting research. The article is available for free download from the Resources page of either Linda's [www.lindabacon.org/resources] or Lucy's [www.well-founded.org.uk/resources] website. Citations not found there can be found in Linda's book, *Health at Every Size: The Surprising Truth about Your Weight*,[3] www.lindabacon.org/haesbook/.)

MYTH 1: Fatness Leads to Decreased Longevity

When it comes to the topic of weight and health, even the "scientific experts" in the U.S. government have a hard time distinguishing facts from biases—or perhaps we should say they have a hard time giving up biases when the facts prove them wrong.

There is by now an enormous amount of peer-reviewed research indicating that people in the "overweight" category live longer than people in the category deemed to be "normal" and advisable—and that people who are mildly or moderately "obese" live at least as long as normal-weight people. Even government statisticians at the U.S. Centers for Disease Control and Prevention (CDC) found this to be true—and, under pressure, published this result in the prestigious *Journal of the American Medical Association*.[4]

Lest people actually allow the data to inform practice, however, the CDC issued a disclaimer to state health agencies, encouraging them to disregard the data. In their words, "Despite the recent controversy in the media about how many deaths are related to obesity in the United States, the simple fact remains: obesity can be deadly." In another document similarly designed to divert us from acting on the radical implications of the evidence, they wrote, "We need to be absolutely explicitly clear about one thing: obesity and overweight are critically important health threats in this country." In effect, the CDC warned us against allowing the evidence to distract us from prejudice.[5,6]

If all it took to change minds was to talk about scientific "evidence," then you'd think the CDC would stand by its own conclusions, wouldn't you? That's what we're up against when we challenge the status quo on weight and health. So if our ideas at first seem preposterous to you and hard to believe and incorporate, that's understandable. You're in good company with many well-established experts.

MYTH 2: BMI Is a Valuable and Accurate Health Measure

Consider BMI, which we are taught to use as a basis for defining someone's health status. When the United States established the standards that it and many other countries currently use, the data the committee examined showed that health decrement didn't occur until there was a BMI of 40, though they set the standard for overweight at 25 and obesity at 30. When I (Linda) queried a committee member about why they set the numbers this way in the absence of supporting research, her response was that they got a lot of pressure to conform to international standards.

Examine those international standards, set by the World Health Organization (WHO), and you will find that the WHO relied on the International Obesity Task Force (IOTF) to make the recommendations. At the time, the two biggest funders of the IOTF were the pharmaceutical companies that had the only weight-loss drugs on the market. In other words, the pharmaceutical industry, which has a vested interest in making us believe that fat is dangerous—and that they have a solution—wrote the BMI standards that are currently used.

> The pharmaceutical industry, which has a vested interest in making us believe that fat is dangerous—and that they have a solution—wrote the BMI standards that are currently used.

The derivation of children's BMI standards was even worse. They were just arbitrarily assigned, without even the pretense of considering health data.

The facts show that many people in the BMI categories of "overweight" and "obese" live long, disease-free lives. In other words, adiposity (fatness) alone doesn't mean sickness. Moreover, when we make health assumptions about people based on their weight, we also miss the many thin people who get "obesity-associated" diseases. Others measures of adiposity, including hydrostatic weighing and bioelectric impedance, waist-hip ratio and waist circumference, are similarly flawed.

MYTH 3: Fat Plays a Substantive Role in Causing Disease

It is true that many diseases are more commonly found in heavier people. However, that doesn't mean that weight itself causes disease. Much of the evidence on the topic is based on epidemiologic research, which is a type of research that tracks people over time and examines differences between groups. And while many epidemiologic studies have shown that larger people are more likely to develop several diseases, it is important to note that epidemiologic research shows *association*, not *cause*.

Consider the difficulties that arise if we try to assign causality to epidemiologic data. Let's look at a less charged association to understand this better. There's a lot of research that shows that bald men have higher incidence of cardiovascular disease (CVD) than men with lush heads of hair. So, do we look at that data and conclude that baldness causes CVD or that hair protects against CVD? No. Examination of other research shows us that bald men have higher levels of testosterone—and that high levels of testosterone increase risk for CVD. In other words, testosterone is a confounder that explains the relationship between baldness and CVD.

Coming back to the association between weight and disease, there are many traits and behaviors that differ between lighter- and heavier-weight people that could explain the increased disease incidence much more readily than fatness.

To just give you a small glimpse, let's take a look at three confounders.

FITNESS

The renowned Cooper Institute in Dallas, which focuses on preventing disease, has been gathering data on a large group of patients. Its follow-up has shown that the death rate for women and men who are thin but unfit is at least twice as high as for their fatter counterparts (those in the "obese" category) who are fit.[7] In fact, across every category of body composition, unfit individuals (and those with chronic disease) have a much higher death rate than those who are fit, regardless of what they weigh. Fitness appears to be a key factor in providing protection, not what you weigh.[8]

> Across every category of body composition, unfit individuals have a much higher death rate than those who are fit, regardless of what they weigh.

DISCRIMINATION

It is tough to live in a higher-weight body in this culture. Stigmatization and discrimination are pervasive and severe. In fact, research shows that the prevalence of discrimination based on weight is now on a par with discrimination based on race and sex.[9] (As we're focusing so much on negative consequences of belonging to a stigmatized group, we don't want to lose sight of the fact that stigmatized identities are also a huge source of positive experiences, such as high self-acceptance and community). Discrimination is stressful to experience, and stress is a risk factor for most of the obesity-associated diseases, including cardiovascular disease and diabetes.

In an interesting take on this issue, researchers asked a group of more than 170,000 U.S. adults their actual weight and what they perceived as their ideal weight. They found that the gap between those weights was a better indicator of mental and physical health than BMI.[10] In other words, body dissatisfaction, or *feeling* fat, has a stronger negative health effect than *being* fat.

DIETING AND WEIGHT CYCLING

Research indicates that calorie-restriction dieting increases inflammation. Repeated cycles of weight loss and regain result in even more inflammation. Inflammation is a risk factor for many obesity-associated diseases, such as heart disease and diabetes.

So it's clear, then, that there are many factors that can explain the association between higher weight and disease that have nothing to do with adiposity itself. As we mentioned earlier, blaming fatness for heart disease is a lot like blaming yellow teeth for lung cancer, rather than considering the possibility that smoking might play a role in both. And telling people they need to lose weight is a lot like telling someone with pneumonia to stop coughing so much—it may not be possible and won't make the disease go away.

As you can see, fat is very much exaggerated as a health risk. We have demonstrated this in two ways. First, we provided evidence that overweight and moderate obesity are not associated with decreased longevity. And second, we showed evidence that although disease is more common among fatter people, factors other than weight confound the relationship and play a causative role.

MYTH 4: Exercise and Dietary Restriction Are Effective Weight-Loss Techniques

In Chapter 2, we discuss in more detail the energy balance equation, otherwise known as the First Law of Thermodynamics, which states that when the number of calories you consume is less than the calories you expend, you should lose weight. While this is a scientific fact, that doesn't mean that diet and exercise—even when they are maintained—will actually result in sustained weight loss. In fact, there has never been a research study that has demonstrated long-term maintenance of weight loss from lifestyle change for any but a small minority. Even the few bariatric surgery studies that have reported long-term data are showing weight regain, though the process is slower than with diet or exercise.

The few lifestyle trials that have snuck through the literature proclaiming success have all had serious methodological or interpretative difficulties. Consider the large, multicenter, government-sponsored Look AHEAD Study, the most recent to loudly proclaim in the headlines, "Proof That Diets Work." The researchers' data do indeed show that after four years there was a 5 percent maintained weight loss.[11] What the researchers don't tell us, but that can be discerned in their data, is that the women are still on their weight-regain trajectory. They had originally lost 10 percent of their weight, and over the four years had been slowly regaining. A better way of interpreting this study is to say that the researchers have slowed the weight-cycling trajectory (which can be attributed to the researchers' intensive monitoring and support, as well as the cherry-picking of participants after monitoring compliance and outcome during a run-in period, a time before the trial began). But it would be more honest if the researchers held off claiming that weight loss can be sustained until the regain trajectory flatlines. What's more, as is typical in weight-loss research, monitoring for adverse effects of any form was notably absent.

Dieting triggers a reduction in leptin, which both increases appetite and decreases metabolism.

When we examine the body's regulatory mechanisms, it shouldn't be too surprising to us that few people sustain weight loss. We can identify compensatory pathways that get activated to try and ensure weight stability. For example, dieting triggers a reduction in leptin, which both increases appetite and decreases metabolism. And chronic dieting results in chronically less leptin release, which could easily explain why the majority of people with a history of dieting actually gain weight over time. They have become hungrier and their bodies are more sluggish.

Yes, some people do lose weight and keep it off—and that perpetuates the belief that anyone can if they try hard enough. Some smokers live to be ninety, but that's not good reason to recommend cigarettes for longevity. The scientific research is very clear on the topic of weight loss—in fact, it's one of the most well-tested experiments in science. The vast majority of people who intentionally try to lose weight will regain their initial weight loss—and biology directs this process.

The vast majority of people who intentionally try to lose weight will regain their initial weight loss—and biology directs this process.

MYTH 5: We Have Evidence That Weight Loss Improves Health

There are endless studies that show short-term health improvements result from short-term weight-reduction interventions. Yet, in all of these studies, the participants are doing something to achieve the weight loss, usually changing their diet or exercise habits. Both of these have been shown to improve health independent of weight loss. So these studies don't prove that the weight loss itself affects health—and they typically don't consider any harm done. A liposuction study that controlled for behavioral change found no improvement in the health problems that get blamed on obesity, despite the weight loss that occurred.[12]

Several epidemiologic studies have evaluated weight loss and health *long term*; they have consistently found that weight loss is associated with *increased* mortality, even when the weight loss is intentional and the studies are well controlled with regard to known confounding factors, including hazardous behavior and underlying diseases.

The reality: (1) Health improvements can occur in people of all sizes, independent of weight change; and (2) the pursuit of weight loss leads to health decrement. One of us, Linda, has shown this in her published research; Lucy's unpublished research and many other studies corroborate this. In case you're wondering why some research claims to be saying weight loss works, check out "Weight Science: Evaluating the Evidence for a Paradigm Shift," the open-access *Nutrition Journal* article on validity in weight research that Linda and Lucy coauthored—all is not as it seems regarding scientific integrity, and it's much worse than you imagined.

MYTH 6: Health Is Largely Determined by Health Behaviors

Diet is but one of many factors that influence health. It is certainly true that, like physical activity, eating well improves well-being not just in the long term, but on a day-to-day basis, too. "Attuned" eating behaviors and activity demonstrably boost

energy levels throughout the day and offer a host of other immediate benefits. ("Attuned" means practices that are guided by
an internal "felt" sense; we'll discuss this in more detail later
in Chapter 3.)

Consider the case of someone whose headaches abate after
she learns she has been chronically dehydrated and begins consuming more juicy produce and drinking more water. Or whose
constipation eases when he seeks out fibrous foods that appeal
to his tastes. Or the possibility that increased intake of omega-3
fats may affect heart health or depression levels.

Despite all this, it is wrong to assume that diet, or even
diet and exercise, are the main determinants of health. In fact,
according to the U.S. Centers for Disease Control and Prevention
and others, health behaviors account for less than a quarter of
differences in health outcomes between groups.[13] What is the
main determinant? The answer may surprise you.

Picture a large corporation with a wide range of job positions
and employees drawn from varied backgrounds. The average
person at the top of the organization can expect to enjoy better
health and live longer than someone in a lower-paid job, even if
they share identical eating and exercise behaviors.[14] It's a myth
that executives are more likely to experience heart attacks than
their subordinates. In fact, people lower on the social ladder usually run at least twice the risk of serious illness and premature
death as those near the top.[15] And not only poor people are
affected: Even among middle-class office workers, lower-ranking
staff suffer more disease and earlier death than their bosses.[16]

So, while diet and exercise can influence self-care and
health outcome, social differences actually account for most of
society's stark health differences.[17,18] In the workplace, the gap
appears to emerge largely from the job strain of low "decision

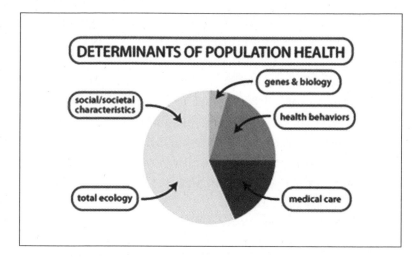

Estimates of how each of the five major determinants influence population health. The absence of a line separating total ecology from social/societal characteristics reflects the lack of quantitative knowledge on these two determinants at this time.[19]

© Centers for Disease Control and Prevention.

latitude"—lacking a say in how you organize your work.[20] In society at large, the stress of being poor and suffering oppression or discrimination (from various causes) leads to worse health outcomes than those experienced by people blessed with greater privilege—health discrepancies that *cannot be pinned to health behaviors*.[21]

> So, while diet and exercise can influence self-care and health outcome, social differences actually account for most of society's stark health differences.

On the basis of Myth 6, most medical and government health recommendations (not to mention innumerable corporate initiatives, ad campaigns, and even reality TV shows) focus on the need for individual change to improve public health, when what's really needed if people are to live better and longer is social change. At the same time, it's important to remember that looking after ourselves can influence our well-being, and that we must support people in finding ways to respond to their needs. There's clearly a place for self-care along with collective efforts to advance equality.

If our basic survival needs have been met, it's our physical responses to life circumstances that prove the key determinant to health. Those well treated by society, who see themselves as valuable and worthy, enjoy a protective cushion that trumps the stress response. By contrast, lives under threat—whether due to poverty; adverse childhood events; noise pollution; damp houses; fear of crime, racism, or sizeism; insecure or dangerous work; or a general lack of control over one's circumstances—trigger stress responses that work overtime and reduce bodily resilience. It is a toxic combination even for those who follow all the best lifestyle recommendations.

Any number of adverse personal circumstances, such as chronic anxiety, insecurity, low self-esteem, social isolation, and lack of control over work and home life, can trigger long-term stress. And in industrialized countries, the lower one stands in the social hierarchy, the more common these problems are.

Almost everyone experiences occasional stress, and this benefits us at times, but what is it about chronic stress that is so pernicious? Under stress, our hormones and nervous system mobilize our "fight or flight" response, raising our heart rate, mobilizing stored energy, diverting blood to muscles, and increasing alertness so we can run from or face up to a perceived threat. These responses are briefly helpful if you find yourself confronting, say, a wild animal or Viking marauder. In modern times, the threats we face are rarely so physical or short-lived. Yet they trigger the same effects on our cardiovascular and immune systems. If those tensions arise too often or go on for too long, we become vulnerable to a wide range of poor health outcomes, including infections, diabetes, high blood pressure, heart attack, stroke, and depression. So blaming "obesity" for these ailments proves, well, mythical. Shifting the health care focus to helping people improve self-care and develop resilience, and working out how to build fair societies that foster a sense of coherence, are two strategies for health that have much stronger scientific backing than eating or exercising for weight management.

MYTH 7: Science Is Value-Free

Scientists are people first, influenced by the societies and times they live in. If we live in a sizeist society, we're likely to bring sizeist views to research and practice. Rather than viewing sizeism as something society has constructed, we likely won't even notice it. It seems the responsible thing to do is to tell people their fat is killing them. It doesn't raise any eyebrows when fat people have their heads cut off in media pictures, sending a message that this body is so shameful that it doesn't deserve a face. The run-of-the-mill images we see accompanying medical stories support stereotypes by showing fat people eating fatty or sugary foods or lounging around watching TV—not swimming, enjoying their veggies, or walking in the park. We take inequalities and substandard science at face value because they align with the dominant "common sense" view. If we have misgivings, we may not want to risk social or professional censure by speaking up. But mostly, we don't even know there's a problem—we're not motivated to ask questions that shed more light on the situation because the answers we have fit with everything we've been taught. So silences and knowledge gaps grow. The huge omission in health and nutrition books of the way that factors besides diet and exercise influence health outcomes is a particularly dangerous example of one of the silences that emerges.

The Cost of These Myths

Trumpeting obesity concerns and admonishing people to lose weight is not just ineffective at producing thinner, healthier bodies—it's downright damaging. Current ideas about weight are the source of our pain, not the solution. They lead to repeated cycles of weight loss and regain, to food and body preoccupation, self-hatred, eating disorders, weight stigmatization and discrimination, and poor health. Few of us are at peace with our bodies, whether because we're fat or because we fear becoming fat. Judgments about fatter people cloud their ability to fully contribute to our world and elevate thin people to an unmerited status. Every time we make fat the problem, these are side effects, however unintended they may be.

Along with the common myths, there are common rejoinders, such as, "I get what you say about everybody deserving respect, and that the majority of people would benefit from focusing on living well for its own sake, but surely people who are very fat do need to lose weight for their health? What if people struggle to get out of the house because of their size? It wouldn't be fair to leave them to it."

It's true that not everyone is at a weight optimal for their health. Whereas both thinner and heavier people get joint pain, for instance, depending on the cause of the problem, joint pain may be exacerbated by weight in heavier people. However, given what we know about dieting, the last thing such people need is to pursue weight loss. Instead, they should be offered investigation that may lead to diagnosis as well as appropriate support for pain management and increased mobility in the same way that thinner people with joint pain would expect their needs for investigation, pain management, and mobility issues to be taken seriously.

Consider the experience of Linda and her father. Linda is slender and her father was fat, and both consulted orthopedic surgeons for knee pain. Linda's doctor suggested that she try stretching, strengthening, and eventually surgery, while her father's doctor instructed him to lose weight. Doctors put him on diets—over and over again. He never developed a regular exercise habit and struggled with weight cycling and disordered eating his entire adult life.

Carrying more weight may have aggravated her dad's joint problems, but the prescription to lose that weight added to the problem and was never a solution. Most people have tried dieting already. It requires a kind of cognitive dissonance to be able to say, on the one hand, "Sure, I accept that dieting hasn't worked," then, on the other hand, say, "Of course, in some cases, you just have to find a way to make it work, because fat is doing damage here." Linda's father could have benefited from the same advice given to Linda: stretching, strengthening, and surgery, plus the option of looking at his relationship with food and weight from new, health-enhancing perspectives.

In addition, we need health care that validates the reality of the situation—and in this sense, while HAES is not weight biased, it is not weight neutral, either. Because of stigma, the place that the condition occupies in fatter people's lives will be very different from that of a thinner person with similar symptoms. If giving an exercise prescription to Linda's father, for example, it would be helpful to acknowledge and explore the impact of stigmatizing messages often found in popular gyms and in other areas of his daily life. A respectful consultation with a health care practitioner will not make patients immune to the onslaught of fat blame and shame and being undeserving, but it politicizes their experience and can be the start of a trusting relationship based on dignity and compassion.

The Paradigm Shift

Health at Every Size replaces this old, discredited paradigm. It seeks to help people treat themselves well in the body they have right now, whether or not it is their optimal weight. For some people, following HAES will lead to weight gain; in others it will lead to weight loss, according to their setpoint weight (which we'll discuss in Chapter 3) and any consequences of an improved relationship with food and their bodies. HAES practice recognizes the value of size diversity and leads us toward a world where people of all shapes and sizes feel respected and are supported in taking care of their bodies.

HAES does not claim that everyone is at a healthy weight. What it does do is ask for respect and help people shift their focus away from changing their size to enhancing their self-care behaviors—so they let weight fall where it may naturally. It also keeps the role of lifestyle as a risk factor for disease in perspective.

The End of the Obesity Epidemic

So, the real weight problem is our focus on treating and preventing fatness. The obesity epidemic exists only because we have defined it to exist. The epidemic will vanish as soon as we stop pathologizing weight and relegating people to baseless and arbitrary categories like normal weight, overweight, and obese as the basis to assess their well-being—which then affects beliefs about people's worth. By encouraging an accurate understanding of the root causes of health, the prevention of stigma, and promoting positive self-care for people of all sizes, we can address real health concerns, giving both fat and thin people the support they deserve, and avoiding devaluing people and worsening the health divide. The change in thinking that underscores HAES emerges from and fosters understanding and compassion, key elements of the real route to health: a just society. HAES puts health—and caring—back at the heart of health care.

> The real weight problem is our focus on treating and preventing fatness.

But What about the Kids?!

The public and media hysteria about the "epidemic" of child obesity has stirred up extreme and emotional responses based on moralizing judgments that spread body hatred and fat stigma. And when we look at the actual data, we find fallacies similar to those discussed for adults. Children's weights are *not* spiraling out of control. In fact, the largest U.S. study, the National Health and Nutrition Examination Survey, has found that their obesity levels have been stable since 1999 (except among a small subset of the very heaviest boys); this is based on the most recent data, gathered in 2009–2010,[22] and is supported by data from all over the industrialized world.

There has never been any real evidence that today's kids will have shorter lifespans than their parents. In fact, all trends show the opposite: Life expectancy continues to rise, overall health continues to improve, and today's kids are healthier than their parents were at the same age.

Diabetes

The "childhood type 2 diabetes epidemic" that supposedly arises from kids gaining weight is also shaky. A study published in the *Journal of the American Medical Association* shows type 2 diabetes to be virtually nonexistent among kids younger than ten years.[23] Examining two million children between the ages of ten and nineteen, researchers found 512 cases of type 2 diabetes had developed over two years. Do the math (or "maths," in British terms!), and this translates to roughly one new case of type 2 diabetes every two years for every 4,000 kids studied. Certainly really unfortunate for that one kid and their family, but is this really an epidemic?

Type 2 diabetes in kids is also rare when compared to other concerns. Consider its ranking among these diseases, and its incidence per 100,000 kids (figures compiled by Jon Robison[24]): autism, 340[25]; cerebral palsy, 240[26]; Down syndrome, 120[27]; sudden infant death syndrome, 56[28]; cancer, 15; type 2 diabetes, 12.[29] As you can see, type 2 diabetes is less prevalent than all of these: only 12 incidences per 100,000 kids.[30] Then, take these comparisons further and factor in eating disorders:

2,900 incidences per 100,000 kids.[31] This means that a child is 242 times more likely to have an eating disorder than type 2 diabetes—yet which of these gets more media attention? And consider this: It is not a coincidence that eating disorders are so high in a climate of fat fearmongering.

Do Fat Children Become Fat Adults?

Another commonly expressed fear is that fatter children become fatter adults. Regardless of whether you consider this concerning, it's a fallacy nonetheless. A review of seventeen studies that tracked groups of children for decades found kids had more of a tendency to slim down over time (50–75 percent of those sampled, across different age groups), and that only 5 to 20 percent of obese adults were obese as children.[32] A study following more than a thousand British families similarly concluded that there was "little tracking from childhood overweight to adulthood obesity."[33] Another study found that 79 percent of the 3,000 thirty-six-year-old obese adults surveyed first became obese as adults.[34]

More Myths about Kids

And here are a few more myths deconstructed:

Myth: BMI is a meaningful health indicator.

Reality: BMI categories were created by looking at American kids' heights and weights in the 1960s and 1970s and then *arbitrarily* defining children above the ninety-fifth percentile as "obese" and those in the eighty-fifth percentile and above as "overweight." We still compare kids to those norms. No scientific reason has been presented for choosing the data from that time period as the norm, nor has a scientific reason been presented for deciding that the top 15 percent should be considered pathological.

Myth: Children are more sedentary than they used to be and this leads to weight gain.

Reality: Most data do not support the assumption that there's a direct link between children's activity levels and weight gain. Besides, the focus on activity as a route to weight management misses the important point that activity is great for children's health and well-being, whatever their size or shape.

Myth: Children put on excess weight because they eat "junk" food.

Reality: "Junk" food is still relatively rare in the countries with the fattest children in the world, such as Egypt and Algeria.[35] Furthermore, research suggests that larger children generally eat fewer calories, not more, than children in the "normal weight" category.[36] Besides, the focus on controlling food as a route to weight management, and weight as a route to health, misses the important point that nutritious eating is great for children's health and well-being, whatever their size or shape.

Myth: Children can't be trusted to regulate their own eating.

Reality: Parents who control their children's feeding behaviors by restriction are more likely to have children who are challenged by self-regulation of energy intake and weigh more as adolescents than their peers.[37] Children who are provided with structure around meals, who are offered a variety of foods, and who are trusted to regulate how much and what to eat develop positive self-esteem, learn agency and self-care skills, and appreciate their bodies and do not become preoccupied with food.[38]

Children's Self-Image

All children are affected by our society's extreme focus on weight, the valuing of thinness, and the conflation of thinness with health, success, popularity, happiness, love, and all good things. Misinformation proliferates, much of it promulgated by dietetic and other medical authorities, making it relatively easy for stereotyping to be accepted without question. High rates of eating disorders and body dissatisfaction in children of all sizes are no doubt in large part fueled by our war against fat (and the values and thought patterns it espouses and rests on).

Many children feel inadequate and insecure in their bodies. All too often, children who don't fit in with the in-crowd experience bullying. Added to this, kids from marginalized groups pick up messages about their social status from a very early age as they see their peers (mis) represented, or absent, from TV shows, magazines, billboard images, and so forth. The current anti-fat climate means that heavier kids hear from every conceivable source that they need to be thin—that there is something wrong with them. Thus fat kids learn they are not okay the way they are. They believe they are unlovable and do not deserve a good life unless they have "perfect" bodies.

Even when parents do a great job loving their kids just the way they are, there is still a barrage of negative messages to contend with from the playground, media, teachers, doctors, concerned relatives, friends of the family, and even clergy. Some U.S. states require public school students to be weighed, and childhood weight monitoring has been introduced in the United Kingdom. The school then sends a note home to parents with the child's BMI and, in some cases, instructions on managing calories for weight control—known to be detrimental. The state of Texas even attempted to ban elementary school students from bringing cupcakes to celebrate a birthday! (We were glad to hear that legislators passed the "Safe Cupcake Amendment" to protect the right of parents to tote cupcakes to school.) And there are laws being debated in the U.S. Congress to allow teachers to rifle through lunchboxes and seize contraband such as potato chips and candy bars. These policies get us obsessed about eating and leave us tripping over food rules. They do more to promote disordered eating and weight concerns than they do to prevent problems associated with poor diet.

Fighting the Stigma

The perpetual stereotyping of fatness affects children of all sizes, with fat children as the direct targets. When fatter kids are bullied, and many of them are, there may be nobody in their lives telling them that the bully is wrong, and that everyone everywhere is lovable just as they are. It takes a strong sense of self-worth to feel safe in your skin in a world where some bodies are dubbed "good and acceptable" and others are dubbed "bad and unacceptable."

We need to make this a world where all bodies are good bodies, where children can feel good about themselves in their own unique and precious bodies in all of their glorious diversity. We have the opportunity to stop this self/body hatred and to help kids learn to respect and celebrate body diversity. By becoming aware of the impact of our words, behaviors, and attitudes around these issues, and the deep structures that underpin them, we can begin to shift narratives and create spaces where children of all sizes know they are loved and respected just as they are.

CHAPTER 2
Weight Regulation

Now that we've deconstructed the war on fatness and the myth of obesity, let's get grounded in understanding the science behind weight regulation. Picture this scenario:

New Year's morning arrives, and Maria awakens to a new year filled with hope and promise. She springs out of bed, heads toward the shower, and decides along the way to step on the scale to see whether the holiday parties have taken a toll on her waistline. The dial settles on a familiar number. Being careful seems to have paid off; perhaps it was worth having invested so much effort limiting her calorie intake after all. On the other hand, she's exactly where she was this time last year when she vowed she was going to push her BMI down into the "healthy" range. She decides then and there that she will resolve in the New Year's Day spirit to change her ways and lose those ten extra pounds. Over the next weeks, she cuts out calories by eating smaller portions and eliminating her early afternoon chocolate fix. She joins a gym and starts to work out regularly. Sure enough, the number on the scale steadily drops. Maria's happy and proud and feels certain that this year she's got her weight problem licked.

Sound familiar? Maria's success at losing weight in the short term is not unusual, and perhaps you've even been there. Any weight-loss plan that helps you to reduce the amount of energy you eat relative to the amount of energy you spend will result in initial weight loss. Thousands of research studies document the short-term success of countless weight-loss programs.

Some weight-loss programs promote special food combinations, such as high protein and low carbohydrates, or low fat and high carbohydrates, or avoiding certain foods, like those containing gluten or sugar; others advise calorie counting or exercising. But the bottom line is always the same: Losing weight is a matter of manipulating calories through diet and/or exercise—and *discipline*.

Seems like common sense—and it definitely works on a short-term basis. But here's the rub: For the vast majority of people, it just doesn't pan out in the long run—and it has damaging side effects. As much as we hate to burst Maria's bubble, odds are she's going to put the weight back on through no fault of her own. Though most people believe dieting to be the right thing to do for weight loss (and health), "common wisdom" has sent us down the wrong path.

Weighing In

Like Maria, many people in industrialized countries begin their day with a ritual weigh-in. Even if you don't do it every day, you can probably relate to what Maria felt when she looked at her scale. But what does the number on the scale actually measure? Because this number has such an impact on how we feel and the choices we make—and because the health care industry certainly takes this number seriously—let's discuss what the number on the scale means.

Your body's biggest component is water—about 60 percent of your weight. Physically, you're like a big water balloon: five quarts (about a liter) of blood and forty quarts of other fluids held together by a bag of skin. Your other major components are muscles and bones—what scientists call "lean weight"—and your fat weight.

In a given day, your weight can fluctuate by several pounds, primarily due to changes in body water. Considering this, you can see that your scale has limitations: Even though it's simple and convenient, the scale is not an effective way to measure *substantive* weight change. If you doubt this, try eating some salty foods—tortilla chips and dip will do. You'll get thirsty, retain water, and "show" more pounds on the scale. Conversely, you can spend a few hours sweating in the hot sun and manipulate your scale in the other direction. The first time you ate, the second time you didn't—yet both times you probably saw dramatic changes in the number on the scale, and in the first scenario, that weight increase was much bigger than the weight of the food.

So, from the perspective of substantive weight, those day-to-day changes on a scale—or the quick, dramatic, short-term weight loss that comes from dieting—are relatively meaningless. Changes in fluid levels can indicate a disease process, such as heart failure, but for otherwise healthy people, fluctuations in weight due to fluid composition don't tell us much more than how hydrated that person is. In other words, sometimes weight loss is just dehydration.

Sometimes weight loss is just dehydration.

To study weight regulation more meaningfully, scientists use a specific measure, "energy." Energy skips right past water and refers to fat and lean body tissues exclusively.

Your Dynamic Body Needs Energy

Your body is in a state of constant flux. Bones lose and gain calcium; cells die and get replaced; hormone levels are constantly shifting; foods are eaten, broken down, and transformed. Even when you're resting, your body is in constant motion internally. It takes energy to make this happen. Just as a car needs gas energy to power its movement, we need food energy for living. (We'll see later that the usefulness of comparing the body to a machine stops here.)

Metabolism: How We Use Energy

"Metabolism" is a term that describes our use of energy. It is popularly thought of as calorie burning—in other words, using energy. The overall speed at which you carry out your metabolic processes is termed your "metabolic rate"; folks who use energy very quickly are said to have a fast metabolism. Conversely, those who seem to gain weight even though they don't eat much are considered to have a slow metabolism; they don't use energy as readily. Scientists use the term "metabolism" to cover a broader umbrella than in its common usage, encompassing all energy reactions in our body, including reactions in which we synthesize substances such as body proteins.

Energy Balance Equation

Energy cannot be created or destroyed—it can only be converted from one form into another. This is an immutable fact, and one of the most important laws of nature. In fact, we referred to it earlier in Myth 4: the First Law of Thermodynamics or the Law of Conservation of Energy.

In other words, when energy intake equals energy use, body energy stays the same (and so will weight, except for fluctuations due to water). Tip the balance, and you lose or gain energy, which will show up on your scale. When you take in more energy than you use, you'll store the extra, leading to energy (and weight) gain, and when you spend more energy than you take in, you have to use some of the energy already stored in your body, resulting in energy (weight) loss.

This has been expressed in a simple mathematical formula, called the energy balance equation:

$$\text{Body Energy Change} =$$
$$\text{Amount of Energy Consumed} - \text{Amount of Energy Spent}$$

Or, to use other words:

$$\text{Body Energy Change} =$$
$$\text{Energy In} - \text{Energy Out}$$

When your combined lean and fat weight is fairly stable over time, you're in "energy balance," despite dynamic flux. If you're gaining weight, it means your energy expenditure or food intake has changed so you're adding more energy to your body relative to the amount you are spending, which is called "positive energy balance." The excess energy gets stored, usually in fat cells. In people who are exercising hard, the energy may get used instead to build extra lean weight (muscle). Weight loss, on the other hand, occurs when you're in negative energy balance. It signals removal of energy from your fat stores (and/or lean weight, like your muscles) to help meet your body's energy needs.

Calories Are Your Friend

Energy is measured in calories (or in the metric system, kilojoules). We need calories because our bodies need energy. Unfortunately, because fatness is feared, calories have a bad reputation in our modern industrialized world—they're thought of as the enemy. As a society, we try to avoid them, and we willingly pay extra for food that's billed as having minimal calories. Making calorie value the main criterion for food selection means we're gladly paying extra for less "fuel value" in effect, and typically sacrificing non-nutritional aspects of eating such as satisfaction and enjoyment. In our drive to eat less energy, we end up supporting a huge low-calorie/"lite"/diet food industry and eschewing an intuitive approach to food that inherently balances pleasure and nourishment.

> We can relate to food and calories as nourishment—as opposed to villains who pack on pounds.

To get a grip on weight and well-being, we need to reframe the role that the calorie has taken on. To start with, we can relate to food and calories as nourishment—as opposed to villains who pack on pounds. The pleasures of eating go beyond physical nourishment to include socializing, nostalgia, and familiar comforts, and the excitement of new experiences (as we try unfamiliar foods).

Energy Balance: Theory vs. Practice

While the energy balance equation is theoretically accurate, it is often misinterpreted and misapplied in real life. One major difficulty is that it sets us up to think of bodies, and therefore people, as machines. This isn't the case, though. For example, someone may eat the exact same food as a friend and get all of the energy from that food. The friend, on the other hand, may have some friendly bacteria in his or her gut that digest some of the energy so that it never gets into the body. Or, perhaps another person doesn't absorb all of the nutrients, and some travel out as excrement. (Stated in other terms: Suppose you and your friend both eat a 100-calorie banana. One of you may absorb 95 of those calories, while the other absorbs 85; the two of you take in a different number of calories, despite consuming the same food.) Or, once the nutrients are absorbed into the body, in one person it may trigger chemical reactions that turn part of the food energy into heat, which dissipates from the body; in another person, that energy may settle into fat stores.

What accounts for these variations in how we absorb or use energy? We could come up with a book-length tome to answer this question, but here are a few examples of characteristics that differ among individuals and result in these variations:

- Hundreds of genes play a role. Some, for example, influence whether energy gets preferentially stored or burned; others influence whether your body responds to chronic exercise by becoming more efficient at burning fat or by increasing your muscle mass. Furthermore, nutrients from the foods you eat can turn genes on and off, and change the speed at which they work. Activity, stress, and other lifestyle factors can also stimulate the production of hormones and neurotransmitters that regulate how your genes are expressed.

- Certain medications, including common antidepressants, antipsychotics, beta-blockers, and migraine medications, cause some people to gain weight. Ironically, many of the drugs used to treat diseases that have been blamed on high weight, such as diabetes and high blood pressure, can themselves cause weight gain.

- Disease processes, such as the insulin resistance that is an aspect of type 2 diabetes, can often result in your body storing more fat and burning less sugar.

- The bacterial makeup of your intestines influences your weight. Some bacteria wring calories out of your meals, while others leave them all for you. Dieting shifts the balance of bacteria so you're likely to absorb more calories from your food, playing a role in the common post-diet weight regain.

- When environmental toxins like plastics build up in your blood, they disrupt your endocrine system in a way that increases fat storage.

■ How you feel about the food you're about to eat, and stress-related gut troubles, can indirectly impact metabolism through altering absorption.

Ironically, many of the drugs used to treat diseases that have been blamed on high weight, such as diabetes and high blood pressure, can themselves cause weight gain.

One result of misinterpretation of the energy balance equation is that when dieters don't lose weight, they get blamed and aren't believed, because the energy balance equation and body-as-machine metaphor foster the expectation that they would drop pounds, and at a predictable rate. The same assumptions affect how patients are treated in health care settings, which seldom allow for the fact that people absorb and use calories in different ways.

So don't be misled: Just because the energy balance equation is accurate in theory, doesn't mean that eating less or exercising more necessarily results in sustained weight loss, or that each individual will have the same response to eating or activity habits. Watch two people eating the same diet: One might gain weight while the other loses. Read on to understand what really goes on with energy balance in the body.

Gaining Energy (Energy In)

We have just one way to get energy into our bodies, and that's through eating and drinking. Food and calorie-containing drinks are described as "potential energy." Only carbohydrates, protein, fat, and alcohol provide energy, and their calorie contents don't vary: Carbohydrates and protein always contain approximately 4 calories per gram, fat always contains approximately 9 calories per gram, and alcohol always contains approximately 7 calories per gram. You can calculate the amount of energy provided by a nutrient by multiplying the calories in a gram by the number of grams in the product. You can then calculate the total amount of energy in a food by adding up the energy from each of those nutrients. Other compounds in food (such as water, vitamins, minerals, or phytochemicals) don't contain usable energy, so they aren't considered when calculating the energy content of foods.

If you compare them ounce for ounce, protein and carbohydrates contain less than half the energy of fat. Water adds weight, texture, and bulk to foods, but no calories. That's why high-fat, dense foods (like peanuts) are high in calories, while low-fat, water-packed foods (like celery) are lower in calories (and crisp and refreshing!). Peanuts are 48 percent fat, 26 percent protein, 20 percent carbohydrate, and 6 percent water. For comparison, celery contains no fat and is 1 percent protein, 5 percent carbohydrate, and 94 percent water. There is a vast difference in calorie content between the peanut and a stick of celery because of the higher fat content and lower water content in peanuts. You get 550 calories in 100 grams of peanuts, compared to only 15 calories in the same weight of celery.

Bear in mind that the reported calorie content of food is an approximate measure. The actual composition of peanuts, for example, varies with season, variety, growing conditions, and so on. It lends an air of scientific precision to see these figures repeated, but they are meaningful only as a ballpark reading.

Also bear in mind that calorie information on food labels is only approximate, and manufacturers are allowed by U.S. law a 20 percent margin of error. Furthermore, though most of the food you eat crosses over the wall of your digestive tract and into your body, some of it is fermented by bacteria or may not be absorbed and is instead excreted in your stool. So even if you know the calorie content of food, you never know exactly how much is getting into your body.

It's also interesting to note that, for all the attention that's been paid to the calorie as a precise scientific standard over the years, the term is technically incorrect. A calorie is actually a very small measure of energy; the correct term is "kilocalorie," which refers to 1,000 calories.

Using Energy (Energy Out)

There are three major components to how we use energy (calories):

- Resting metabolism
- Activity
- Digesting, absorbing, and processing food

RESTING METABOLISM

Most of our energy goes to maintain unseen functions in the body; we need a lot of energy to keep our bodies' complex processes cranking. Every second you are alive, your bone marrow is making 2.5 million red blood cells to keep your body supplied with oxygen and nutrients and to tote away cellular waste. Your brain is processing information through its trillion nerve cells, each connected to a hundred thousand others, helping to ensure that your heart beats and your lungs expand and contract. That madly whirring brain of yours is the most energy-hungry of all organs. Even at rest, our brain is using about 20 percent of the body's energy, ten times the rate of the rest of the body! (This is what makes the brain so vulnerable—cut off its energy supply for just ten minutes and you get permanent brain damage.)

The rate at which we use energy for these vital functions is called our "basal metabolic rate." Because it is so difficult to measure the energy consumed for basal metabolism (survival functions) alone, scientists frequently use a more expansive term, "resting metabolism," which includes all of the energy consumed when one is in a resting state (e.g., lying down or fairly still). Resting metabolism is typically the largest component of energy use, accounting for about 60 percent to 70 percent of the average person's daily energy use.

Each person has a characteristic resting metabolic rate. You use energy at a different rate than anyone else, even when you are doing nothing. The largest determinant of someone's resting metabolic rate is the amount of muscle tissue they have. That's because muscle is very active and requires a lot of energy to sustain. A large, muscular man has a higher resting metabolism than a small woman. Fat tissue, on the other hand, is relatively inert and requires very little energy to sustain—which means it doesn't contribute much to resting metabolism.

You may have been born with the ability to burn a lot of energy quickly and effortlessly, while others have a "sluggish metabolism" and don't use energy at a very fast rate.

Many factors other than your size, fat, and muscle tissue figure in resting metabolism. Some are genetic and immutable. You may have been born with the ability to burn a lot of energy quickly and effortlessly, while others have what's called a "sluggish metabolism" and don't use energy at a very fast rate. It's interesting to consider the cultural value judgment in using the term "sluggish"; from a scientific perspective, the person with a slower metabolism is much more efficient, a trait that would have been highly prized in earlier times when food was harder to come by.

ACTIVITY

Activity is the second-highest calorie burner for most people. This category includes intentional exercise, such as running or jumping, as well as any activity your body performs beyond your resting metabolism, including unconscious activities (such as transmitting nerve messages as you read this page) and conscious movements (such as writing).

Activity accounts for about 30 percent of the average person's daily energy use, although of course that varies tremendously. A young woman training to run a marathon may expend more energy on activity than she does supporting her basal metabolism, but it may take only 15 percent of his energy to fuel the daily activity of a sedentary older man.

DIGESTING, ABSORBING, AND PROCESSING FOOD

It takes a lot of energy to metabolize the food you eat, including the energy used for digestion, absorption, transport of nutrients, and storage or use, typically accounting for about 10 percent of the energy you use in a day.

Some foods require more energy to process than others, and yes, this means that you can boost your energy use through your food choices. Protein stimulates your metabolism a little more than carbohydrates, and both of these stimulate your metabolism far more than fat, resulting in extra calories burned.[1,2]

Also, it takes a lot of energy to convert carbohydrates and protein into fat and store it in fat cells. In theory, at least, if you ate a large number of calories from a high-carbohydrate, high-protein meal, you would store fewer calories as fat than if you had eaten an equivalent quantity of high-fat foods. And calories consumed all in one meal require less energy to process than if the same quantity had been spread out over several meals. So grazing—eating smaller, more frequent meals—also results in more calories burned.

In reality, however, trying to manipulate your energy spent on processing food won't help in weight regulation; its effects are small and your body is quite effective at manipulating intake and expenditure, overriding attempts at cognitive control.

Weight Regulation in Action

Wasting Energy: The Elusive Uncoupling Protein

What if someone could just burn off extra energy from the body without doing anything? It is possible, and in fact the average person wastes about 7 percent of energy every day. Scientists call this "adaptive thermogenesis." A substance called uncoupling protein (UCP) made in fat tissue is the go-between. This protein essentially uncouples the burning of fat from energy production, meaning that when you burn fat, you create heat that dissipates from your body but no usable energy.

Some people make more UCP than others, and the amount made plays a large role in body size. If the gene for making UCP is very active in a person, he or she will have a faster (less efficient) metabolism than others and is likely to have less body fat as well.[3]

As you can imagine, scientists have examined UCP extensively in their efforts to find a magical weight-loss technique. They've studied mice and found that ones bred with a specific UCP gene, human UCP3, ate more than control mice, but were thinner, even though their activity levels were the same. One study showed that UCP3 mice had only half as much body fat even though they ate as much as 50 percent more than normal mice.[4]

Given the high demand for, and money involved in, weight-loss strategies, scientists are hard at work trying to figure out what activates the genes that create UCP. The answer to this question could help find a way to trigger this gene in people for whom it is less active and rev up their "sluggish" metabolisms. Of course there's no way of knowing at the moment what the health consequences of altering someone's gene expression in this way might be.

One way to activate the gene that directs the body to make UCP is to eat a lot of food. When some people eat large quantities of food, their body compensates by making more UCP, thus burning off the excess calories. They can eat major amounts without gaining weight, but it only works for some people. On the other side of the fence are those who make less UCP and are more likely to gain body fat when they eat a lot.

Fuel Efficiency

The human body is remarkably efficient at using energy. It doesn't take much food energy to power us. Suppose you wanted to run a marathon (26.2 miles). Depending on your conditioning and several other factors, you would burn about 100 calories per mile, or a total of 2,600 calories to fuel the run. A car, on the other hand, may be able to travel those 26.2 miles on a gallon of gasoline, which is the energy equivalent of about 31,000 calories.

Think about it: A car needs twelve times as much energy! Viewed in another way, if cars converted energy as well as our bodies do, they could get 300 miles per gallon.

Too bad we can't build a car that's as fuel efficient as the human body. We would celebrate that. But where thinness is prized, this level of efficiency is seen as a problem, as it's one of the main reasons some people gain weight so easily.

Your Personal Metabolism: An Elusive Measurement

Do you wonder how much energy you use in a day? This can be calculated with a fair degree of precision by using high-tech lab equipment that measures the amounts of certain gases you exchange with the environment. But it's impossible to come up with an accurate number through mathematical formulas because of the high degree of variation among people and the impossibility of accounting for all the contributing factors. This is where our car analogy ends! Using formulas for energy requirement can also get in the way of feeling comfortable around food choices and listening to your body. You don't need to know how many calories you burn in a day to help you regulate your weight. Formulas can be useful, even vital, when calculating nutritional requirements in clinical situations, such as for a burn victim or someone being tube-fed, but outside of this arena, they will likely cause more harm than good.

> You don't need to know how many calories you
> burn in a day to help you regulate your weight.

The average person consumes one million or more calories per year, yet weight changes very little in most (non-dieting) people. What this tells us is that energy balance is regulated with a precision of greater than 99.5 percent.[5] This clearly far exceeds what someone can consciously monitor. (Even more so when you consider allowable margin of error on food labels!) The trick in weight regulation lies in relying on this unconscious, or intuitive, regulation. There's a lot to gain when people give up on calorie counting. More on this in Chapters 4 and 9.

CHAPTER 3
Weight-Loss Realities

So now that you know the basic theory behind weight loss and weight gain, it should be easy to lose weight, right? After all, based on what we looked at in Chapter 2, due to the First Law of Thermodynamics, weight loss appears to be the result of simple math: Eat fewer calories than you use. Diet and/or exercise plans based on this idea are effective for short-term weight loss. On the other hand, whenever the body has excess calories it converts them to fat, saving them for a rainy day, and so weight inches up. Thus the common weight-loss prescription to eat less and/or exercise more *seems* logical enough. But hang on—we also seemed to be saying there's more nuance involved in the science, such as UCP, and reason to doubt efficacy long term. Yet surely potential confounders can be outwitted, and failure can be overcome with willpower. So, is there evidence diets work long term? Nope!

That's because we're not in conscious control of how the body uses energy. Attempts to manipulate the energy balance equation, like eating less or increasing activity, may be met by compensatory adjustments. The human body has a fairly complicated built-in weight-regulation system that can override conscious efforts to change weight. For example, suppose you cut calories. In response, your body could slow your basal metabolism, resulting in fewer calories burned. This means that you can actually *gain* weight in response to cutting those calories!

We're not in conscious control of how the body uses energy.

The news that our bodies can undermine efforts at weight control is actually good, because it also demonstrates that your body is enormously successful at regulating your weight. It's not something we need to "work at"—in fact, this "control" approach ends up being counterproductive. Healthy bodies will maintain a stable weight, if we leave them to it. It's worth pointing out here that healthy bodies will always come in a range of shapes and sizes. So saying that eating to one's appetite means someone will stabilize at their healthy weight isn't the same as saying everyone who does this will be thin.

While the First Law of Thermodynamics is always upheld, the conventionally discussed contributors to your body weight—such as what, when, and how much you eat, as well as how you expend energy (including your inclination to move)—are not completely under conscious control. Moreover, bodies are not machines and do not respond in consistent, predictable ways to foods and nutrients ingested. Energy and nutrient metabolism is influenced by a whole host of interrelated factors and varies among people and within the same person, according to circumstances.

Your Setpoint Weight

As discussed in Chapter 1, on a short-term basis, you can often control contributors to the energy balance equation, and short-term weight loss is relatively easy. But long term, your body is unlikely to let you get away with this. Within each of our brains lies an incredibly powerful mechanism to control our weight: a somatic body-fat control center that works tirelessly to maintain weight at a level that it (not your conscious mind) decides is appropriate—your "setpoint weight." To manage your setpoint, your body may respond to the energy deficit that dieting creates by turning on physiological processes designed to conserve weight. Part of this may include intense hunger signals; in addition, you may feel less resilient and energetic than if you were well nourished, which can also affect eating choices and activity levels.

Your setpoint weight is the weight range that your body likes best. It is governed by a section of the hypothalamus (with help from a few other areas) that sends signals to manipulate your eating and activity habits and metabolic efficiency. But don't confuse setpoint and weight associated with "normal" BMI, which we'll discuss more later in this chapter. People in any population will always come in a range of weights. In a group where everyone eats to appetite, we'd expect some people at the lower range of the BMI scale, more in the middle range, and others at the higher weight range, each at their own setpoint.

To understand what is meant by your setpoint, consider the following scenario. You are out for an afternoon stroll, enjoying the warmth of the sun on your back. Without any thought or effort, you begin to sweat, which lowers your body temperature and keeps you comfortable. Suddenly, dark clouds sweep over the sun. Again, your body adjusts for you, causing you to shiver, thus raising your temperature. All of this occurs without any conscious effort on your part, right? Now, imagine if controlling your weight could be as effortless. Well, guess what? It can be!

Homeostasis: An Internal Thermostat

"Homeostasis" refers to your body's innate ability to maintain relatively stable internal conditions despite constant environmental changes. Without this monitoring system, you would die.

Consider body temperature, for example. Your body must stay within an acceptable temperature range to survive; you simply can't tolerate internal extremes of hot or cold. That's why specific physiological mechanisms keep your body temperature hovering in a range that's acceptable.

The hypothalamus is a structure near the base of your brain that monitors the temperature of your blood. When you're exercising vigorously, your body heat increases. Warm blood coursing through the hypothalamus triggers the release of hormones and nerve signals that enlarge the diameter of blood vessels in your skin. As the volume of blood moving through these vessels increases, it carries the heat to the surface of your skin, where it dissipates into the environment, resulting in your cooling off. You'll start sweating, and as the sweat evaporates it transfers heat away from your body.

But what if you go out scantily clad in cold weather and your core temperature drops? Again, the hypothalamus registers this. This time, it sends nerve messengers that trigger shivering, which generates more heat to raise your body temperature. You'll also have learned to put another layer on, get a hot chocolate, and find a heating vent!

Many other physiological variables (oxygen and carbon dioxide levels, blood volume, blood glucose) likewise must be tightly regulated. For each, your body will accept a certain range. Physiologic mechanisms keep you humming along and prevent disastrous dips or curves.

Calorie Counting Works Against Your Body

Your body is strongly invested in helping you maintain homeostasis, including a relatively consistent amount of body fat, and it has efficient mechanisms that pull off this amazing feat. Paradoxically, issues with weight regulation often start when we try to take over the process of weight control by aiming to be a certain weight and following food rules to try and reach that weight. This leads to a troubled relationship with food, body (self) hatred, and metabolic responses to inadequate nourishment and stress. The result is escalating weights and poorer health, not slimming down, and not greater well-being. Among people who "eat normally," which at its simplest means eating to appetite and with no undue concern about weight, the body will regulate around its setpoint and achieve weight stability with remarkable efficiency. That is why many non-dieters can maintain stable weights effortlessly.

> Among people who "eat normally," which at its simplest means eating to appetite and with no undue concern about weight, the body will regulate around its setpoint and achieve weight stability with remarkable efficiency.

Consider, for example, a fifty-year-old man who weighs approximately five pounds more than he did when he was twenty. If he eats about 2,000 calories per day, over the course of those thirty years he will take in about 22 million calories. Five pounds of body fat is the equivalent of about 17,500 calories, which means in mathematical terms he was only 0.08 percent off in balancing energy in versus energy out. (That means his body was over 99 percent accurate in matching energy use to energy intake!) This amounts to a difference of about 50 calories per month—less than the energy contained in one egg. Doing the calculation demonstrates the vast figures involved over time, and provides ballast for those nervous about loosening control over food rules and leaving such a seemingly huge undertaking to "eating to appetite." Remember, in reality, the body is a skilled regulator when it's allowed to be, as long as it's not treated as a machine.

The concept of homeostasis is especially important when it comes to weight regulation. We repeat: How much body fat you maintain is tightly regulated within a certain range by complex physiological mechanisms. That your body is strongly invested in keeping you at a certain weight isn't particularly radical or new news from the research laboratories. More than fifty years of research support the homeostatic regulation of body weight, and it's commonly accepted by scientists.[1] Your body is savvy—don't underestimate it!

Your Fat Thermostat

Your setpoint is controlled similar to a thermostat. Imagine that you set your home thermostat to 65 degrees. Every thermostat is programmed to maintain a certain acceptable range. Let's suppose that your range is 4 degrees. This means your temperature control system won't get too aggressive as long as the house stays between 63 and 67 degrees. However, if the temperature drops below 63 degrees, the heat turns on strongly, bringing the house back into the setpoint range. Likewise, if it gets hotter than 67 degrees, the air conditioning comes on.

A certain amount of body fat suits your brain, and it likes to stay in that ballpark range.

Your body fat setpoint works much the same way. A certain amount of body fat suits your brain, and it likes to stay in that ballpark range. Your body fat sends constant signals to the control center that regulates your setpoint, keeping it abreast of the existing state of your fat stores. These signals go out every moment, which means your brain is constantly aware of even tiny fluctuations in fat stores. Your brain pulls together these fat-store messages with other relevant information, and responds by cueing body processes to maintain your setpoint. It's a finely tuned process that is really robust. It means that if you generally eat to appetite and are comfortable with your body, you enjoy moving it within any limits you may have, and you look after yourself in other ways, then you're at your setpoint, which is your healthy weight. This could be anywhere along a spectrum from thin to fat—and not necessarily in the "normal BMI" category.

Finding Your Setpoint

How can you get acquainted with your setpoint? First, let's identify some of its markers. Your setpoint is:

- The weight you normally maintain, when you eat to appetite
- The weight that results from behavioral and metabolic responses to signals of hunger and fullness
- The weight you maintain when you don't fixate on your weight or food habits
- The weight you return to between diets (which creeps up the more you diet)
- A result of your biology, biography, and current circumstances

No physiologic measure can determine your setpoint, nor can any objective test figure out how tightly yours is regulated. (Scientists estimate that the average person has a setpoint range of about ten to twenty pounds.[2]) The only way to zero in on your setpoint is by trying a radical new diet summed up in three words: Just eat normally!

> The only way to zero in on your setpoint is by trying a radical new diet summed up in three words: Just eat normally!

When you try to control your weight consciously (by dieting, for example), you disrupt your body's internal regulation signals.

Chances are, if you are determined to control your weight by watching calories, you're above your setpoint, not below. While the bottom of your setpoint range is tightly regulated, physiologic mechanisms at the top tend to be far more flexible. As a consequence, it can be easy for many people to override the "fullness" signals, overeat and gain weight, and rise above their setpoint.

What Dieting Does

On account of this setpoint flexibility at the upper end, repeated dieting not only disrupts the signals, but ultimately *raises* your setpoint. This section will explain how, over time, dieting ends up being counterproductive as a weight-control technique— analogous to throwing gas on a fire to put it out. There are many other ill consequences caused by dieting and the "thinness equals health" dogma that promotes it, which we'll discuss later.

Most dieters experience this familiar scenario: the exhilaration of initial weight loss followed by a drive to eat, leading to weight regain, guilt, and despair. Many who have been through the diet cycle repeatedly also report post-cycle weights disappointingly higher than their pre-diet number.

Shame and self-blame are common responses to this familiar "diet-fail" scenario—not surprising, given our society's sizeist stereotypes, judgmental messages on fat, and the entrenched idea that there's robust research showing dieting works (there isn't). Failing to lose weight long term is a sign of the success of your internal weight regulation. So diet failure is no more a sign of gluttony or "lack of character" than breathing deeply after exertion indicates lung failure, or shivering in cold weather evinces weakness.

> Diet failure is no more a sign of gluttony or "lack of character" than breathing deeply after exertion indicates lung failure, or shivering in cold weather evinces weakness.

For anyone who overeats after ending a diet or finds his or her intake gradually trickling up, it's a normal and predictable physiological reaction to what the body perceives as "starvation." You can only "cheat" biology so long, before recovery mechanisms kick in.

Let's look more closely at what really happens when we try to diet or exercise to lose weight. At first, the calorie deficit often has its expected effect: Since your body isn't getting sufficient energy to fuel its needs, it burns energy already on your body (your carbohydrate or fat stores or perhaps the protein that is part of your muscle, immune system, or other body parts). The energy loss shows up as weight loss on the scale.

But don't be fooled. Your body is paying close attention, and notices the fat loss (mediated by the hormone leptin). If the fat loss exceeds the amount that is comfortable and healthy for you, your body will try to replace your fat stores. One mechanism is to bump up your appetite to get you to take in more calories. (Who hasn't experienced an insatiable appetite when on a diet?!) Not only will you be thinking about food more frequently, but your satiety mechanisms will be weakened, and your tastes will change so that a wider range of foods is now appealing to you.

But we all know that some dieters have strong willpower, and some may be able to ignore their hunger and maintain their diets. For some people, the hunger signals may even dissipate at some point; their body turns off hunger signals because they waste energy it's trying to conserve. At that point your body could initiate other compensatory processes, some of which are beyond your conscious control. For example, perhaps your heart rate slows slightly. (Ever wake up in the morning with less get-up-and-go than usual? This may just be the result of a metabolic slowdown to conserve energy.) Or perhaps your body doesn't fine-tune temperature regulation as precisely. The shifts will be small and slow, and may just contribute to that oh-so-common weight regain.

Rather than being an indelible character trait or personal failure, post-diet compensatory eating comes as a direct consequence of the dieting itself, our bodies' nearly irresistible biological compensation triggered by weight loss. Accusations of personal failure ignore this science and are value judgments based on stereotypes or blame-ridden interpretations of behavioral counterreactions to starvation.

Being Fat Does Not Mean You Overeat

The cultural narrative is that heavier people overeat. If your weight has been fairly stable, however, you're probably not overeating at all, although you may hear and believe that you are. Several studies, including the largest health and nutrition study conducted by the U.S. government, the National Health and Nutrition Examination Survey, document that *higher-weight people eat no more than lean people*, despite the popular misconception.[3,4,5,6] One review examined thirteen studies, and found the intake of heavier people to be less than or equal to thin people in twelve of them.[7] In one study, investigators unobtrusively observed customers at fast food restaurants, snack bars, and ice cream parlors, and found that the fatter customers ate no more than thin ones. Many studies support these results, and few show otherwise.[8]

Clearly, humans do a great job of unconsciously (or intuitively) regulating how much energy we consume to match what we expend. Even when the body is over- or underfed, it tenaciously seeks its setpoint. We'll say it again: Eating and energy expenditure are directed by physiologic mechanisms beyond our conscious control that influence metabolism and behaviors. Of course there's also a range of other influences on why we eat what we eat.

Sometimes Your Body Is a Slacker

The thermostat comparison showed that whenever you lose weight and get to the bottom of your setpoint range, your body kicks in regulatory mechanisms that try to pump your weight back up; likewise, when you get to the top of your range, your body's mechanisms press for weight loss. We mentioned before that for most people, this regulation is very tight at the bottom but relatively lax at the top; in other words, weight loss triggers a stronger response than weight gain.

From an evolutionary perspective, this makes sense. Not too long ago, at least in terms of evolution, food was hard to find, and people spent much of their day in search of nourishment. Food was a primal drive: People had to eat when they could get their hands on food—or die. It helped to have genes that encouraged eating and allowed people to conserve energy and store fat, and it makes sense that we developed genes and regulatory processes that get us to eat. That's why food tastes good. It has to reward us in some way, or we wouldn't keep eating.

To better examine this motivation, researchers surgically altered a mouse and completely removed the reward systems in its brain. With no pleasure associated with eating, it lost interest and had to be fed by tubes to survive. So it seems reasonable to say we have evolved to enjoy the taste of food. Fat appeals particularly because it's loaded with calories to sustain us, and we evolved to like sugar because it gives us quick energy. This biological drive becomes more insistent when we're over-hungry—one reason that dieters can feel so out of control around sugary and fatty foods, leading to cravings and claims of sugar addiction. Satiety response is also weakened, compelling us to eat more calories. When our body systems and conscious motivations are more confident about food availability, these drives aren't so intense.

Other "thrifty genes" have also evolved to help our bodies store fat during times of plenty and conserve energy when food is scarce. When food shortages were common, people at greatest risk were the ones who burned energy quickly and couldn't store fat. So it naturally follows that those who survived to pass on their genes—our ancestors—were the proud possessors of thrifty, energy-storing genes. In the past few centuries, however, our environment has changed radically. Food is plentiful and more people spend time at desks or on sofas than gathering nourishment. Those same fat-storing and fat-saving genes that saved our lives are no longer essential. The world we have created is very different from the one we were designed for.

Other environmental changes have accompanied increased food availability. Wherever food is not readily available, hunger drives people to eat and satiety (or supply) puts the brakes on. Now that the supply for many nations is less limited, different uses of food, such as soothing emotional hungers and bonding us socially, take on greater significance. In industrialized countries today, most people eat (or don't eat) based on psychosocial factors, not physiologic ones (although the increased use of food banks in the United Kingdom and the United States shows a recent increase in people living with food scarcity). When food is secure, cognitive control of eating behavior intersecting with emotional influences is now the norm, whether that means you're consciously trying to control your food intake or eating beyond fullness.

In other words, we now have a genetic propensity to store energy, absent the food shortages that prevent overnutrition. This wouldn't be a big deal except that many of us no longer allow physiology to regulate our food intake: We eat in the absence of biological hunger, and don't allow feelings of fullness to register and push us away from the table. Adding to our weight-gaining propensity, we've grown into a sedentary society and less often trigger the biochemistry needed to mobilize our fat stores and keep our weight-regulation system sensitive to appetite cues. But a word of caution—remember, we're making sweeping observations that apply at the level of populations. It's not the same as saying people are fat or thin according to how much they eat or exercise, or that fatness is always a sign that something has gone awry in metabolic regulation. What we are saying is that at a population level we're programmed to gain weight, and food insecurity, cognitive restraint, and other factors amplify this tendency.

In fact, the diet culture itself has spawned yet another weight-gain vector, the consequences of repeat, or "yo-yo," dieting. In times of plenty, the thrifty genes that spur us to store extra fat would normally lie dormant. However, the yo-yo-dieting body views deprivation as starvation. Repeated dieting, therefore, sends the thrifty genes into overdrive, raising your setpoint. Yo-yo dieting habituates your metabolism to store *extra* fat as soon as a diet ends, in preparation for the next perceived shortage. Dieting thus becomes one of the quickest routes to long-term weight *gain*.

Dieting thus becomes one of the quickest routes to long-term weight *gain*.

With all of the evidence stacked up, it's easy to see why so many of us are above our setpoints or raising them, leading to larger waistlines.

Putting the Body Back in Charge

Beneath the weight gain spawned by these cultural changes, however, our bodies still have internal mechanisms for regulating a healthy setpoint weight. (There are minor exceptions to this, including people with genetic mutations like Prader–Willi syndrome that lead to defects in regulation of satiety and metabolism.) The answer lies in ceasing our habit of overriding these fail-safes—and getting back to the basics of letting our body do the job of regulating our weight.

The key is to switch goals: Instead of continuing the deprivation-waging, frustration-inducing uphill battle called dieting, make it your new intention to look after and enjoy your body (and life!). A side effect of this will be improved health and weight regulation.

Why do we all have different setpoints? We might as well ask why we are different heights, as the answer is the same. (Think about why we ask one question and not the other.) There are several components to your setpoint: genes, metabolic inheritance, your life-course (to be examined in Chapter 5), and current lifestyle (including medication). We're going to look in most detail at current lifestyle, but we'll start by explaining the other factors.

While we attempt to tease apart the variables by way of explanation, the reality is that body weight is a (shifting) end point for an inherently linked and interacting set of factors including generational effects, food intake, activity, metabolism, endocrine control, and genetics.

It's in the Genes

Researchers separate the effects of genes from lifestyle habits by studying families. Results vary, depending on how the studies were conducted and what types of relatives were studied. But the consensus among the largest and most influential studies is that, among factors affecting our weight, genetics represents about a third of the total influence. For example, the two most comprehensive studies, with twins, adoptees, and nuclear-family members as subjects, suggest genetics alone accounts for 25 percent to 40 percent of the weight variance between individuals.[9,10,11] Many studies attribute an even larger role to genetics, suggesting that it accounts for 50 percent to 90 percent of the variance.[12] Inheritance plays a large role not only in how much fat your body maintains, but in where and how you carry it.[13]

Some studies try to tease out the effects of genetics versus environment on weight. Adopted children have weights very similar to their biological parents, but there's little or no correlation between the weight of the adoptees and their adoptive parents, showing biology as a bigger player than upbringing.[14] Body weight in fact proves more heritable than almost any health condition[15,16,17]—greater than breast cancer, schizophrenia, heart disease, and others.[18]

The commonly held belief that anyone can lose weight by eating less and exercising more is at odds with this compelling scientific evidence that weight is, to a significant extent, genetically determined. Consider a study in which researchers put twenty-eight pairs of identical male twins on a six-week high-fat/low-carbohydrate diet, followed by a six-week low-fat/high-carbohydrate diet. In each pair, one twin ran an average of thirty miles per week more than the other.[19] Despite the extreme differences in physical activity, each twin experienced similar changes in weight and blood cholesterol. Exercising more had no effect on weight—further evidence that the body has a genetic setpoint that it is determined to maintain. Consistent with other studies, variability emerged only when the men were compared to men who were not genetic matches.

Although genes wield a large influence on weight, they of course don't present the entire picture. For example, one study compared twins separated at infancy and raised in different homes. These identical twins had similar, but not identical, body sizes and shapes.[20] Even with identical genes, twins' weight can vary, sometimes dramatically.

It is estimated that lifestyle factors can explain an average weight gain of seven to ten pounds per person in the 1990s in the United States.[21] (How are you doing with letting go of obesity myths? Did you just read the weight gain as a problem, or did you read it as a value-free statement?!) However, it is genetics, not lifestyle, that mainly accounts for why we differ so much in size and body type. Less understood but increasingly scrutinized in recent years is the effect of the environment—that the average weight has increased in recent decades in industrial nations clearly shows that something other than genes matters, as genes cannot evolve that quickly.

The Pima Indians' experience offers evidence of the interdependence between our bodies and the environment. The Pimas originated in Mexico, and about a thousand years ago, some moved to Arizona, establishing a community there. The Mexican Pimas are of average weight, while the Arizona Pimas have the world's highest reported prevalence of fatness.[22] If genes alone controlled the scales, both sets of Pimas would be similarly sized.

But if environment alone were the answer, everyone in Arizona would be fat and there would be a standard distribution of weight across the population in Mexico. What can we learn from this? Put simply, it's the gene-environment combination that counts. Pima Indians have an insulin-resistant gene that is weight sustaining, and in a somewhat oversimplified manner it gets called a "fat gene." This provided survival advantages for populations subsisting, as the Mexican Pimas did, on a low-carbohydrate, high-protein diet with periodic starvation. The control mechanism preventing starvation trumps appetite control mechanisms, predisposing Pima Indians to weight gain when they're not starving. If the family is poor, the food culture that emerges, and the impact of chronic stress on metabolism, compounds the likelihood of extra weight gain (as we will explain in Chapter 5, "Health at Every Size: The Body Politic"). The concept of metabolic inheritance helps capture this gene-history-environment matrix. It can explain why first-generation immigrants to the United States are heavier than their peer group: Children predisposed to store energy are more likely to survive in conditions of calorie scarcity and to gain weight with relative calorie abundance (a heightened stress response is also potentially involved).

Increasing Your Gene-Sense

One of the most common misconceptions about genetics is that genes alone account for specific tendencies, like breast cancer, shyness, or fatness. But the reality is not so clear-cut. Yes, we all have genes that regulate a tendency to get cancer, or to be shy, thin, or fat. But just having a gene doesn't mean it's active. For example, suppose two siblings have a gene that predisposes them to melanoma (skin cancer). One spends extensive time in the sun, which triggers expression of that particular gene and increases the likelihood that she will get skin cancer. However, her brother limits his sun exposure, and though he has the gene, it remains dormant.

Another misconception is that traits arise from single genes. In fact, most traits, including weight regulation, are the result of multiple genes. Your specific combination, as opposed to any individual gene, determines your proclivity to weigh what you do. Except in rare cases, no single "obesity gene" is a precursor to being fat, nor is there a single gene that confers thinness.

The genetic heritage you receive from your parents sets the stage. However, the activity of those genes is malleable. Many factors affect activity of the genes involved in weight regulation, such as maternal nutrition, eating, activity, stress, and sleep habits, for starters. As an example of how this works, nutrients from the foods you eat can turn genes on and off and change the speed at which they work. Activity, stress, and other life-style factors can also stimulate the production of hormones and neurotransmitters that regulate how your genes are expressed.

The message is this: You have some degree of power to regulate your genes, but less than most people believe. Both nature and nurture play a role in adult weight (and health).

> People who are motivated to change behavior with the goal of weight loss rarely succeed, whereas those switching their focus to health gain, or attuned living, more often see results.

It's worth reiterating that people who are motivated to change behavior with the goal of weight loss rarely succeed, whereas those switching their focus to health gain, or attuned living, more often see results. Keep the distinction in mind when we look now at altering gene expression.

How can you alter gene expression?

Fighting Setpoint: A Losing Battle

Doing battle with your setpoint in the pursuit of weight loss almost always ends badly. The process is fraught with health pitfalls and emotional costs, and is more likely to result in weight gain than weight loss. Humans come in diverse shapes and sizes. Some are genetically hardwired to be thin or fat with genes so powerful that their bodies resist the influence of environmental and lifestyle change. Others may have genes more susceptible to environmental and lifestyle changes.

For most, the truth lies somewhere in between: Our genes permit a limited range of body size, and our lifestyle habits determine where we will be within that range. Of course there can be a whole heap of reasons why our lifestyle isn't what we'd like it to be—finances, troubled eating, body shame, unsafe neighborhoods, unemployment, and even work schedules (shift work is known to influence health habits, for example) can all affect eating patterns and activity levels in the real world. Food insecurity (not getting enough to eat) also spurs abnormal metabolic responses and behavioral patterns that may lead to weight increase. And when we expand our understanding of environment to embrace social encounters, this opens yet another window on what influences our metabolism.

More useful than asking whether nature or nurture determines weight, we can view weight, like other complex traits, as a heritable *susceptibility*—and see that thinness or fatness manifest only under certain conditions. And a constant theme in all this science is that it better serves well-being and peace of mind to find new ways of relating to food, appetite, activity, and physicality, rather than focusing on weight.

We've begun to explain why, even if you do try to go against nature's plan for your body, your success at making lifestyle changes is partly determined by genetics. Watch two people on a weight-loss program, eating the exact same diet and exercising the same amount; one may lose weight while the other stays the same. In the past, experts chalked up their different results to differing degrees of compliance. No matter what the non-loser reported, he or she was suspected of simply failing to follow the program. What we're saying is that blame laying no longer looks warranted; experts now recognize that the ways people respond to weight-loss regimens are genetically determined.

Given the same weight-loss program and full compliance, different people show different results (unless, as we've seen, they're identical twins).

There's more evidence, too. Consider another twins study, in which twelve pairs of identical male twins were induced to overeat, adding an extra 1,000 calories to their daily diet 6 days a week for 100 days. As you would expect, each twin showed results similar to his brother's, in both weight gain and distribution of fat. What was remarkable was the degree of variation from pair to pair: In one set of twins, each man gained only nine pounds, while in another, each gained approximately twenty-nine pounds! (Incidentally, when these same men were remeasured four months later and five years later, all had returned to their pre-study weights; in other words, once restored to their normal diets and lifestyles, they returned to their setpoints.)[23]

In other experiments, identical male twins exercised on stationary bicycles twice a day, 9 of 10 days, over either 22 days[24] or 100 days.[25] Diets were consistent, and the exercise caused them to spend an extra 1,000 calories. Just as in the aforementioned study, each man's weight loss and change in body-fat distribution resembled those of his twin but not of the other men observed. Another example is the United States government–sponsored Look AHEAD intervention, where Hispanic participants lost less weight than non-Hispanic white participants, despite similar rates of compliance.[26]

Listen to Your Body, Not Poor-Quality Science

Remember, even if you follow all the conventional recommendations for weight loss, you don't get a guarantee that you'll get the weight outcome you want, the health gain you expect, or a result similar to your friends'. You might already know that the outcome is more likely to be one of food preoccupation and body dissatisfaction. But the good news is that there is something to replace this weight obsession, something demonstrated— through sound science—to improve nutritional status and have a positive effect on your sense of self-worth and overall well-being. Importantly, it also sets in motion a way of thinking that challenges size stereotypes and popularizes a worldview that advances a fairer and more compassionate society in which our worth as humans isn't derived from the size of our bodies or how well we fit in with dominant groups. This translates to a win-win for personal and community well-being; as you change your focus you'll learn to appreciate your body and improve how you take care of yourself. Your body will stabilize at its natural weight and you'll be free of the diet cycle. This new practice of acceptance helps you move away from the limitations of the black-and-white thinking that leads to unjust societies, and the mechanistic thinking that tries to make sense of our humanity, and health, by conceptualizing us as machines.

SECTION 2
Reconstructing Respect

CHAPTER 4
Health at Every Size: Personally Speaking

Given what we learned in Section 1 about how body weight gets regulated and the costs of maintaining obesity myths, one sees clearly that it's time to end the war against fat. Beyond what we know from science, perhaps the most compelling reason to call a cease-fire is the damage we cause by doing battle with our own bodies and others'.[1]

It doesn't have to be this way. The Health at Every Size approach offers an alternative that helps us be at peace in our bodies and supports people of every shape and size by helping them find compassionate ways to take care of themselves.

Guiding Principles

The basic guiding principles of HAES are as follows:

- **Respect** (including respect for body diversity.)

- ■ **Critical Awareness**
  - ■ Challenges scientific and cultural assumptions
  - ■ Values people's body knowledge and their lived experiences
  - ■ Acknowledges social injustice and that disadvantage and oppression are health hazards
- ■ **Compassionate Self-Care**
  - ■ Supports people in moving toward:
    - ■ Mindfulness (nonjudgmental attentiveness)
    - ■ Attuned movement, eating, and other self-care strategies

HAES Works: The Evidence

Our own research and experience demonstrate that people can make significant health improvements when they stop dieting and learn to trust their bodies, and that this is more effective than dieting in promoting well-being.[2,3,4] Consider research conducted by Linda and her colleagues, which is consistent with all other research conducted on HAES. We compared "obese" women on a typical diet with others on an HAES program. Both groups of women received support of comparable quality, but the focus was different. The HAES program supported the women in accepting their bodies and listening to internal cues of hunger, fullness, and appetite. After two years, the HAES group sustained improvements in blood pressure, total cholesterol, LDL (low-density lipoprotein), and depression, among many other health parameters. The typical-diet group, on the other hand, showed initial improvements in all of those parameters (and weight loss), but returned to their starting point within a year.[5] The HAES group improved their self-esteem and reported feeling much better about themselves at the program's end, while the dieters' self-esteem plummeted. Also noteworthy, 41 percent of the diet group dropped out of the program (typical of diet programs), while almost all (92 percent) of the HAES group stayed with the program.

The premise of eating what you want and getting healthier may sound foreign to you. In fact, the idea that you can stop watching your calories and eat what you want, when you want, is so contrary to current ideas that it evokes tremendous fear. Some health care practitioners and researchers express concern that these aspects will result in indiscriminate eating and weight gain. One of Linda's colleagues was so doubtful that she insisted on testing the participants' blood lipids and blood pressure three months into the study, and that we be prepared to stop the research if we noticed these measures worsening. As Linda expected, the research shows this concern to be unfounded.

> The idea that you can stop watching your calories and eat what you want, when you want, is so contrary to current ideas that it evokes tremendous fear.

We believe this is true because once participants realized they could eat whatever they wanted and were supported in choosing foods they fancied, and in letting food serve many roles, food stopped holding as much power over them. For example, they didn't have to binge on ice cream because they knew that it would be available to them whenever they desired it. They could put it away when their taste buds toned down and it stopped tasting as good, which resulted in eating smaller quantities (which is more consistent with stable blood sugar regulation). It gave them permission to meet their needs and to eat delicious meals, and it got them out of the cycle of eating surplus and then regretting it. So they began to identify and respond appropriately to their needs, to feel more in control around food, and to become more trusting of their bodies' internal regulation. Rather than eating with abandon—as had been the case with off-limit foods when dieting—they ate with attunement. It is dieting, not HAES, that needs to carry the label, "Warning! Likely to lead to indiscriminate eating."

They were choosing foods that helped them to feel better, too. For example, most started out with typical fast food habits and, like many people, were frequently constipated from the lack of fiber, and felt the bloat and tiredness commonly experienced from the energy-dense meals. After experimenting with a higher-fiber diet, they realized that it made them feel better— bowel movements were more comfortable, and they felt more energized and mood-stable throughout the day. This motivated them to make health-enhancing, feel-good choices.

Participants also got more creative while shopping, in the kitchen, and in restaurants, experimenting with different foods and food preparations, and finding wholesome foods they loved. It's easier to make changes when you are choosing foods you desire than when you are avoiding foods you consider off-limits.

> It's easier to make changes when you are choos-
> ing foods you desire than when you are avoiding
> foods you consider off-limits.

The HAES research clearly shows that it is possible to dump the obsession with food and weight, and the self-hatred and shame about your body. You can reclaim the joy in eating—and it can markedly improve your health and how you feel!

Let's look at the big picture of how you can personally implement HAES thinking. In subsequent chapters we'll look more specifically at nutrition that nourishes, minding your body, and valuing your emotions.

Putting HAES into Action

STEP 1: Accept a Body's Weight!

Challenge those damaging beliefs about needing to change your weight and discover the difference in how you feel. Accepting yourself involves learning to steer clear of the fixation on trying to alter weight and starting to accept your body as it is, right now. Remember, weight is not a measure of someone's worth. Remind yourself of the truth about dieting. (Admit it, you don't need us to tell you it doesn't work long term!)

This is not about giving up, nor does it mean that your body or health is never going to change; rather, it's about moving on from dieting—something that doesn't respect diversity or improve well-being—to embrace something that does. Look out for your needs, and try to meet them. Shift your emphasis to happiness and healthy living, things that *are* achievable. The reality is there's no way of telling if these changes will alter your weight or not. But you know what? As you learn to trust yourself more and respect your body, what you weigh won't be a chief concern.

The emotional dimensions of this shift can take time. As much as you "get it" intellectually, there are likely to be times when you just wish you were thinner and your emotional knowing seems to be playing catch-up. That's okay. You're okay. Change takes time; go easy with yourself as you ride out the conflicting feelings. It helps to remain curious and to replace the old dieter's default of beating yourself up with a new attitude of treating yourself well.

Here are some tips to improving body image:

- Throw away your scale. Or put a sticker with the word AWESOME over the dial.

- Think about how you treat your body. Then compare this to how you would treat a friend.

- Be kinder to yourself! Pamper yourself: hot baths, massages, a head rub. . . .

- Talk to your friends about your feelings. You'll find that you're not alone.

- Enjoy your body. Use it. Find activities that are fun for you.

- Take the time and money you would have spent on dieting and spend it on fun, supportive activities instead.

- Get more media savvy so the sizeist images you see don't bother you so much. Don't beat yourself up when they do.

■ Find ways to limit the damage of unfair comments and treatment—talking, journaling, blogging, activism, joining an online community.

■ Surround yourself with images that reflect diversity, including people of your body size. You don't have to buy into a culture that tells you that there is something wrong with you! (For example, go to an art gallery and look at the range of images of people portrayed in the artwork.)

■ Remind yourself: There is no obligation to rank beauty, conventional or otherwise, as a must-have characteristic. You don't need to be anything other than who you are, whatever that is just now.

■ Identify activities you've been putting off until you're thinner. Start doing those things now!

STEP 2: Eat Mindfully and "to Appetite"

Find out what happens when you aim for mindful, pleasurable eating and shift regulation to your body.

■ Dump the diet mentality and all notions that some outside expert or rule can helpfully tell you what to eat.

■ Learn to recognize what physical and emotional hungers feel like. How are they linked for you?

■ Tune in to what you need and want—be it chocolate fudge cake, celery, or a hug.

■ Take your food preferences seriously—try to match what you want to eat with what you actually eat whenever possible.

- ■ Experiment with stopping when you are full or the food stops tasting as good, knowing there's more where that came from when you want it.

- ■ Be curious about any guilt or shame when you eat more for the sheer deliciousness of food and pleasure of eating. What are your emotions telling you?

- ■ Lighten up on eating rules. Learn to trust your appetite to adjust to instances of eating more or less than you physically need. Pay attention to old fears that get evoked in the process and treat yourself kindly.

This is a slow learning process. Focus on:

- ■ How you feel in your body and emotionally
- ■ Your satisfaction level
- ■ Choosing appropriate foods that keep you satisfied until your next meal or snack
- ■ Being kind to yourself

Address emotional eating. Check out Chapter 8 on "Emotional Empowerment" for strategies.

- ■ Ask yourself, am I physically hungry?
  - ■ If the answer is no, ask yourself:
    - ■ What am I feeling?
    - ■ What do I need?
  - ■ If the answer is yes, eat!

Take special care of yourself. This is a time to be kind to yourself, not come down on yourself. There might be a period of chaotic or unusual eating. Curiosity is a great dinner pal as you make sense of things.

STEP 3: Get Moving, for All the Best Reasons

- **Old model:** You have to *work* out for weight control.
- **New model:** Move for the *fun* of it! (It becomes play, time out—not workout!)
- Move, stretch, and breathe for the feel-good and fun of it!
- Mind the body more holistically.

To gain health benefits, an activity:

- Doesn't have to be vigorous
- Doesn't have to be continuous

Tune into your body so you get more skilled in knowing what to do and when, to feel good. Check out Chapter 7, "Enthused to Move," for suggestions for more active living. What can you add that you would look forward to, and that would make you feel more generally vital?

STEP 4: Use Your Mind-Body Knowledge of Nutrition

We're fascinated by nutrition science—maybe you are, too? We're not going to try and put you off it, but having witnessed the damage dehumanized science has done, we want to urge you to temper the "facts" with your own body wisdom and experience. That way you'll have a useful range of information to help you make sense of things. Remember, too, to use nutritional knowledge in the service of enjoying life and optimizing your well-being, not as a slave to weight control or out of a sense of duty to be healthy. Check out Chapter 6, "Eating Well," for details.

Again: Eating in response to your own embodied knowledge can be fun and nurturing. Don't make the mistake of allowing your cognitive knowledge about a food's effect on weight or health override your felt sense of what you really want to eat and enjoy. If you do "get it wrong," cut yourself some slack; it's all part of learning.

Happy people make wiser choices!

STEP 5: And the Rest: Build Resilience and Sleep Well

As with other dimensions of health, the way events affect us and how we manage stress are influenced by our life experiences and by how society treats us. Equality is a better solution to reducing blood pressure than stress management classes! So if you find you get more stressed than most folks, you don't have to judge yourself harshly or feel bad about it. Instead, why not give yourself a break, remembering that however much of a struggle things are, you are doing your best right now? After all, if you could manage anything better, you'd sure as hell be doing it! Alternatively, is there someone who can bear witness to your anger or validate your experience for you?

Try and find some time for yourself to spend in a way you find relaxing. In addition, talking about what's on your mind with a confidant can be a huge relief. You'll feel better for sharing and being heard in the immediate term (and benefit from the relaxation response).

And be sure to factor in sufficient sleep. Several research studies show a relationship between sleep deprivation and decreased release of hormones that help regulate metabolism and a sense of well-being.

Another twist: Don't self-blame when you're not able to get enough sleep. Don't beat yourself up for being stressed! Practice accepting that you're doing the best you can, however far removed that is from what you think you "should" be doing.

Educate Yourself

There's more background on self-care habits, like eating, moving, and managing your emotions, in Section 3. Where we've given suggestions, use them in a "test and see" way to learn if they're of any use for you. You'll soon discover what works and be able to add your own ideas for self-care. Personally and professionally, we've benefited enormously from working with key HAES principles of attunement and kindness, and we know how they can enhance quality of life, so we're keen to pass on this message. We're also keen on HAES not being misread as simply another self-help program. Equality in health outcomes, and being at peace with ourselves and each other, will come from equality in society, and compassion. There's a bigger picture to well-being than self-help. So a vital piece of the HAES jigsaw involves going from the personal to the panoramic and thereby getting a sense of how life experiences affect our body, behaviors, and health. We'll explore this expanded view in Section 3, which means going beyond conventional theories of "health behavior change" to consider how life circumstances have an impact on our worldview and, in turn, have a bearing on our impetus for, and confidence in, self-care.

CHAPTER 5
Health at Every Size: The Body Politic

The last chapter introduced the rationale for adopting a HAES approach in relation to lifestyle. We considered science that gets neglected when formulating weight-loss recommendations. We listened to how people felt about their bodies and took note of what happened over repeated dieting attempts. This more inclusive approach to evidence, which can be thought of as "integrative listening," is also of paramount importance in drawing attention to factors other than lifestyle that impact well-being and disease. Integrative listening makes for good science, a science that brings evidence on social justice into health care.

Within the past century, the leading causes of death in industrialized countries have shifted from communicable diseases like pneumonia and tuberculosis to chronic ones like cardiovascular disease and diabetes. As these diseases have become more common worldwide in line with rising prosperity, they've become known as "diseases of affluence." They often get blamed on a "nutrition transition" radiating outward from North America into developing countries, spreading disease through the menaces of dietary fat, high-fructose corn syrup, and weight gain. It's true that we've gotten fatter and our diets have transitioned. But the irony is that we're living longer and we've never been healthier. Often a leap is made that erroneously extrapolates causation from these changes in weight and diet. But as we'll see, there's a lot more going on.

We're All Right

How many times have you heard that today's is the first generation of children that will have shorter lifespans than their parents? This proclamation comes from an opinion piece published in the prestigious *New England Journal of Medicine*.[1] No statistical evidence was presented to support the claim, yet you would never know that from the authority it has been granted in the media.

Before you, too, fall prey to hype like this, consider this: U.S. life expectancy has increased dramatically in *the same time period* in which our weight rose, rising from an average 70.8 years in 1970 to 78.7 years in 2011, and continues to hit record highs.[2] U.S. government statistics predict that the average kid can now expect to live eight years longer than his or her parents.[3]

> U.S. government statistics predict that the average kid can now expect to live eight years longer than his or her parents.

Not only are we living longer than ever before, but we're healthier than ever. Chronic disease is appearing much later in life,[4] and death rates attributed to heart disease have steadily declined during the entire spike in population weight.[5] Both the World Health Organization[6] and the U.S. Social Security Administration[7] project life expectancy to continue to rise in coming decades.

Class, Not Mass, Matters

Within this trend of life expectancy gains, however, another pattern emerges: Longevity and health are distributed unevenly among the classes. In short, good health rises in sync with socioeconomic success. Even among groups where everyone has enough to eat, lives in a warm house, has safe work, and has an opportunity to get sufficient sleep and exercise, we see a gradient in health along class lines. This social gradient doesn't just point to illness among poor people—it also points to differential levels of illness among the relatively wealthy who are stratified by status.

This same health gradient has since been found for virtually every disease in every industrialized country in the world. Whether measured by income, formal education, or job status, there is a socioeconomic gradient to health. And the greater the inequality in a society, the steeper the gradient. The United States has the greatest inequality of all wealthy nations—and the greatest health disparities.

> Good health rises in sync with socioeconomic success.

When we consider the growing evidence that life conditions help determine longevity, weight, and health, the role of everyday nutrition and other lifestyle choices diminishes. Even dramatic changes in diet, it seems, may not manage to overcome the influence of circumstances beyond our immediate control, like economic status and living environment. There are many people who eat well and nevertheless suffer from diseases blamed on poor nutrition. Social determinants play a much larger role than we give them credit for in most diseases that we blame on weight or lifestyle behaviors (if we give them credit at all).

This is not to deny that sound nutrition impacts our day-to-day well-being, and may help reduce individual risk for disease and improve the ability to manage or reverse it, but in most cases, there's a far bigger picture contributing to disease risk and disease reduction.

Social determinants play a much larger role than we give them credit for in most diseases that we blame on weight or lifestyle behaviors (if we give them credit at all).

There are by now thousands of studies that track health outcomes to social determinants. Despite these data, the popular perception remains that disadvantaged populations get sick mainly as a result of bad genes or because they lack the character and knowledge to eat right, exercise more, and abstain from smoking or excessive alcohol consumption, even though neither is true. Similarly, most people still believe it's the top executives who are dropping dead from heart attacks, when in truth, as we noted in Myth 6, it's their subordinates. Genes and lifestyle contribute to only a fraction of the class differences in health, and lack of job autonomy accounts for many more deaths than does executive stress. When we talk about the social determinants of health, we're referring to factors beyond genes and lifestyle that influence people's health and are largely out of their immediate personal control. As is the case with low job autonomy, these factors frequently get left out of the picture in traditional explanations of disease. Other vectors of illness include racism, homophobia, sizeism, transphobia, and classism—the list goes on, but these vectors are not usually accounted for in medical or nutrition texts. Once we understand the centrality of oppression and chronic stress in causing many weight-associated diseases, a different set of responses becomes not only possible but necessary.

When we focus solely on an individual's weight or health habits, we overlook structural and political issues that affect health and well-being. Blaming illness on behaviors stops us from addressing the policies and systems that shape our lives in unequal and unhealthy ways. The way that inequalities are systemically woven into the normal operations of dominant social institutions is known as "structural inequality." Structural inequality hides bias and leads to differences in outcomes that are avoidable.

This doesn't mean we need to throw the baby out with the bathwater; helping people take care of themselves—their body, emotions, relationships—is valuable. But health behavior and personal resilience are only one part of the picture. Increasing equality of opportunity, providing education and training for better jobs, investing in our schools, caring for the environment, giving people more control over their work—these are health-promoting strategies, too, and will have more significance for tackling health disparities than getting more people exercising, eating well, and avoiding smoking.

Making Sense of Public Health Inequalities

To give you a better sense of how inequality plays out in health, let's focus on metabolic syndrome, the constellation of health problems most often attributed to high weight and poor lifestyle habits.

Metabolic Syndrome

Metabolic syndrome is diagnosed when someone has at least three of the following: high blood pressure, high blood sugar, low HDL (high-density lipoprotein), high triglycerides, and a high waist circumference. People with metabolic syndrome are more likely to get cardiovascular disease and diabetes and have strokes. Metabolic syndrome is particularly relevant to our discussion, as its occurrence—and the occurrence of the disorders just mentioned—is widely attributed to poor lifestyle choices and/or fatness. Conventional treatment and prevention of all of these disorders focus on weight loss and improving eating and exercise behaviors.

Metabolic syndrome tracks socioeconomic status far more faithfully than it tracks health behavior. Put simply, if you're poor and/or subject to discrimination and the other stressors of an underclass, you are more likely to be sick, even if you eat well and are regularly active. Hardship and discrimination are so clearly parallel to metabolic syndrome that it has led to the condition also being called "oppression syndrome." It would be easy to assume (and many do) that poor people get sick because they eat poorly and are too sedentary. But even when health behaviors—and BMI—are controlled for, the health discrepancies persist.[8] (In other words, consider two people who eat the same, weigh the same, and are similarly active. The poorer person is more likely to get sick than the more affluent person.)

One group of researchers suggests that health-related behaviors account for only 5 percent to 18 percent of neuroendocrine differences that lead to metabolic syndrome.[9] Another team reports similar findings, and explains that "although reducing the prevalence of health risk behaviors in low-income populations is an important public health goal, socioeconomic differences in mortality are due to a wider array of factors and, therefore, would persist even with improved health behaviors among the disadvantaged."[10]

A study involving more than 170,500 U.S. women and men investigated the impact of four factors on mortality: abdominal girth, physical activity, smoking status, and a Mediterranean diet score. They found that even when those factors were "high-risk," they only accounted for 33 percent of the premature deaths, leaving two-thirds unexplained by factors usually targeted in health promotion.[11]

And it's not simply socioeconomic status that impacts health differences; discrimination in any form is a health hazard. Racism, for example, harms health. There are high rates of hypertension among black Americans, and across socioeconomic classes, that can't be explained by genetics or lifestyle alone—but can be explained by experiences of, and responses to, racism.

Status Syndrome

You probably didn't realize that when your mother graduated from college, she increased her lifespan, and set the stage for you to live longer as well. Or that a friend with a slightly higher-status job than yours is likely to live longer and be healthier. But these and other differences in social status—such as education, job title, income, living environment, relationships, social networks, knowledge, and access to power—have a potent impact on health. We used to believe that advances in medicine and technology were the key to our increased lifespans and ability to manage disease, and that social inequalities were an added indignity exacerbating the real health challenges. But we've since realized that we were looking at the problem backwards—it is the social inequalities that are the major cause of ill health.

It is the social inequalities that are the major cause of ill health.

This effect, in which social position influences disease risk, is called "status syndrome," a term coined by Michael Marmot, who has conducted extensive research on the topic.[12] Our status influences both our exposure to stress and our internal response to stress. The issue is not simply one of income, though it is important to consider the realities of material deprivation. Nor is it differences in lifestyle—whether you smoke or eat a daily doughnut. It is the experience of inequality—how much control you have over your life and the opportunities you have—that plays a profound role in health and longevity.

Stress

The lower one's position in the social hierarchy, the greater the exposure to stressful life events such as job insecurity, eviction, crime, sickness, and death, and the larger the impact of these events on well-being. But even the ongoing hassles of daily life are more formidable and stressful in disadvantaged neighborhoods than in wealthier neighborhoods: dealing with low-performing schools, inconsistent and time-consuming public transportation, unresponsive or overaggressive police, lack of childcare, disrespectful supervisors at work, and so forth.

"Stress" is a medical term that describes the body's response, through hormonal and other endocrine changes, to adverse stimuli in the environment. The classic example is the "fight or flight" response: If a tiger were to appear behind you right now, your body would respond by releasing both adrenaline and adrenocortical hormones so you could hotfoot it out of the area. Once the immediate crisis had passed, your circulating hormone levels would return to normal and homeostasis would be restored, no harm done. Turn on the stress response for a minute and it can save your life. But turn it on for twenty years, as we'll discuss soon, and that stress sets you up for a long list of diseases.

"Stress" is also used in a slightly different way to refer to external influences, or stressors, that affect our health. For example, people living on a busy main road will experience stressors of air and noise pollution (which may in turn have an impact on the family's sleep and activity levels). Air pollution damages arteries by provoking inflammation, alters heart function, and has other adverse effects. Chances are that families living in highly polluted areas are in the lower income brackets, so they not only experience more environmental stressors but also have a greater exposure to adversity and fewer protective resources to draw on.

Exposure to pollutants is only part of the picture of how our neighborhoods have an impact on our health. Accessibility to healthy foods is another factor. It's easy to find grocery stores with fresh produce in wealthier neighborhoods; poorer neighborhoods tend instead to have more convenience stores, fast food restaurants, and liquor stores. Also, wider car ownership among the wealthy means that if a nearby store in an affluent neighborhood runs out of what residents desire, they can still get what they need by driving to another store; for residents of poorer neighborhoods, who rely on public transit, travel can be an added barrier to access. It's often less safe to walk or play in poorer neighborhoods, and they may have less green space and natural beauty. In other words, there is a strong differential in how one's living environment impacts the reality of "choice" and affects our ability to engage in self-care and care for our families. It becomes apparent that people who really do have meaningful choices about what to eat and whether to exercise are also privileged by wider social determinants; for many people detrimentally affected by social determinants, the "healthy choice" may not be about whether to have whole-grain or processed wheat products, but be about whether to eat or stay warm.

Social Determinants: A Conceptual Framework

To understand how disadvantages interact and intersect, let's look at five concepts that describe how social factors influence health outcome:

- ■ Allostatic load
- ■ Life-course

- Lifeworld
- Sense of coherence
- Sense of agency

Allostatic Load, a Key Measure

Our bodies constantly experience stress, whether it's from ordinary day-to-day events like getting out of a warm, cozy bed, or from something more abrasive, like getting fired from a job. In chronic (as opposed to acute) stress, the body loses its flexibility in responding to environmental challenges, and biological systems fail to return to homeostasis. Persistent physiological dysregulation may lead to secondary health problems associated with metabolic syndrome, such as atherosclerosis, insulin resistance, hypertension, and immunosuppression.[13]

"Allostatic load" refers to the cumulative collective factors that influence an individual's ability to cope with difficult circumstances. Genetics, personality, previous metabolic strain, and early developmental events all interact to influence physiological and psychological resilience to stress. For example, people who have experienced abuse, neglect, or other forms of early adversity have weakened immunity and are predisposed for heightened physiological reactions to stressful events. (There's a lot of room for change, though, as we can "rewire" our neural pathways to a great extent with the right support.) Those who experience more secure attachment and less exposure to early adversity are generally more resilient.

Allostatic load gives us a way to talk about the impact of chronic stress on metabolism that also takes into account an individual's history and social positioning. It can be used to measure health decrement between groups that poverty alone cannot account for.

Life-Course and Lifeworld: A Broader Approach

A *life-course* approach helps us integrate this information in a meaningful way. Rather than taking a snapshot of somebody's health status in relation to current health behaviors, a life-course approach takes the view that, from conception to death, we accumulate insults and benefits that impact our health.[14] (Allostatic load describes that accumulation.)

Rather than studying health behaviors or nutrient intake in isolation, it makes sense to think of lifestyle habits as part of a system of interlinked effects, including behavioral, psychosocial, genetic, developmental, structural, economic, political, and environmental factors. Their cumulative impact can foster health or disease, and vary according to how an individual experiences stress-provoking adversity, such as poverty, abuse, and discrimination.

The concept of "lifeworld" describes the reality of a person's life. It's our personal sense of the world, made up of all our life experiences, where our emotions are played out and our feelings are expressed (or not), and where we experience the social structure in the form of opportunities, barriers, difficulties, and disadvantage.[15] The concept can be useful for capturing the fact that people's bodily response to physical and biological stimuli occurs within the context of the social environment; it's not as simple as "Y event happens, therefore Z response predictably follows for everyone."

For some people, the lifeworld is a very hostile place—after all, their personal world is where their experiences of discrimination, pain, and suffering reside.[16] Their lifeworld may set them up for diminished health outcome and distress. A classic illustration of this is the finding that institutionalized children with access to similar diets grew at different rates depending on whether they were tended by warm or stern caregivers.[17]

The effects of stressful experiences during childhood may be particularly potent and enduring. The term "biological embedding" of early childhood experience refers to the physiological changes seen among children who face social adversity and the ways in which early experiences can determine whether favorable or unfavorable genes are expressed or suppressed. In other words, our genetic makeup is not necessarily our destiny. A person may only experience the adverse health consequences of an unfavorable genetic makeup if he or she is exposed to unfavorable conditions. (Of course, plasticity has also been recognized: Individuals can often, with effort, reverse this biological embedding.)

Several measures used to calculate risk of heart disease now incorporate knowledge relevant to lifeworld (and status syndrome). Along with standard questions on age, sex, medical history, and so on, the QRISK, a U.K.-based survey to determine individual disease risk, asks for place of residence.[18] In this way the impact of social positioning on health outcomes is taken into consideration in clinical decision making about heart disease. The developers note:

> For non-U.K. use, if the postcode [zip code] field is left blank the score will be calculated using an average value. Users should note, however, that CVD [cardiovascular disease] risk is likely to be under-estimated in patients from deprived areas and over-estimated for patients from affluent areas.

Using this calculation, increasing my (Lucy's) weight by a third does not alter the score, but a simple move from a high-status neighborhood to a poor one doubles the risk projection.

Likewise, the Scottish Index of Multiple Deprivation uses about thirty-one variables to assess socioeconomic status, many more than conventional instruments.[19] It shows that leaving deprivation out of risk assessments for heart disease potentially denies treatment to those who need it most, allocating the most deprived areas only 50 percent of actual need.

Sense of Coherence and Sense of Agency

Researcher Aaron Antonovsky was interested in why some people fared better than others in conditions of extreme stress—very extreme, in fact, as he worked with adult survivors of the Holocaust.[20] Rather than focusing on disease, Antonovsky asked, "What keeps people healthy?" In answer he proposed the concept of "sense of coherence." This can be understood as the extent to which people feel confident that they can reasonably influence how things will turn out. It means the world seems predictable and explicable, that they have the optimism and resilience to cope with what they face, and that they believe that it is worthwhile to make the effort to get through any challenges. More recently, the experience of emotional closeness has been added to the list. We know that across a group of people coping with the same circumstance, those who have a strong sense of coherence will fare better in terms of health.

Being able to make sense of what's going on, and expecting to receive fair rather than undeserved poor treatment so you can exert influence, is also part of a "sense of agency," an expression that describes the feeling of being able to act in your own life to make a meaningful difference.

In his studies of civil servants in England, Marmot, whom we met in the Status Syndrome section, showed that workers lower on the job hierarchy are much more likely to become sick from stress. His research indicated that what workers experience depends not only on the demands made upon them, but also on whether they perceive that they have the power and resources to cope with those demands. High-level executives usually do. But power and influence over one's life—that is, a sense of agency—decreases as one goes down the income scale. The lower individuals are ranked in the hierarchy, the less access they have to the money, power, status, knowledge, social connections, and other resources needed to manage and gain control over their lives.

Also striking in Marmot's study is that none of the participants are poor in the conventional sense. We're used to thinking that poverty is bad for health, and so it is. But even people in the lowest grades of British civil service are not poor in the absolute sense of the word. Yet a gradient existed, and it was not simply about poverty. This gradient has been found not just in Britain but also in the United States, Australia, Canada, and Scandinavia.

A lot of what we're talking about boils down to the exercise of power in relationships. This is not just about the workplace: It's about where you are in the hierarchy and how that relates to the circumstances in which you live and grow up, as well as work. In some ways, then, we can say that relationships are key to well-being, and social networks are indeed a significant factor in buffering stress. In a meta-analytic review, covering more than

300,000 people, high social connectedness and social integration confer a 50 percent to 90 percent increase in survival.[21] Quite remarkably, the degree of mortality risk associated with lack of social relationships is similar to that which exists for more widely publicized risk factors, such as smoking.[22] Several experiments are now demonstrating that when families and communities have the resources and power to take more control over their lives, their health improves.[23,24] This doesn't exonerate us from reducing poverty; however, it does show the limits of an individualistic lifestyle-change model of health.

Each of these concepts—allostatic load, life-course, lifeworld, sense of coherence, and sense of agency—helps build a vocabulary that enables us to talk in ways that link the personal, sociopolitical, and physiological. They make it more possible to talk about ways in which people internalize power and knowledge, leading to health ramifications.

How These Factors Work Together

We've looked at stress and oppression mainly through the lens of social status and size stigma, with some reference to age, gender, disability, and other traits associated with discrimination. The term "intersectionality" is used to describe the way in which different axes of oppression do not act independently of one another but are interlinked. Sex and gender provide us with good ways to explain how intersectionality and structural inequality affect health. There are considerable differences in mortality and morbidity between men and women and genderqueer people, both globally and within nations. Biology explains some of these differences, but not all; it is mediated by an interaction between gender and other axes of power. For example, research conducted in a population of American female nurses finds that the health risks associated with fatness are very high when compared to a population of women in less affluent non-Western cultures. This study shows that size, sex, ethnicity, socioeconomic status, and other axes of power interrelate to influence experiences of self and stigma, so that women in different cultures experience stigma differently. As a side note, it is also interesting to observe that the health risks associated with fatness in women are higher in cultures that value thinness and support dieting.

Human Rights Abuses

It is important that we keep in mind the impact of discrimination on people's lives, not only because it affects health but because it points us to human rights abuses. Good health for all will come from tackling material and social deprivation and promoting equality. There can be a benefit in helping people reduce the harm of embodied inequality—for example, helping larger people learn ways to protect themselves psychologically when they are insulted by a stranger, or to stand up for themselves when they are insulted at the doctor's office; or helping people find new ways of coping with emotions that might ordinarily trigger their starve-binge cycle or induce them to drink at unsafe levels. That said, it is vital we all keep sight of the fact that while personal care can improve the quality of people's life and their sense of well-being, structural change is needed. Fundamentally this is a human rights issue, albeit one that supports health equality. It provides a new understanding of health, one that undoes the conventional frame of individualism and allows for the value of connectedness, in which social justice is central to health and well-being.

Many people struggling with food and weight issues benefit from hearing about HAES, which is wonderful. We want to keep this healing in sight and also hold on to the need to validate the central role of respect and fairness in advancing equality, health, and good science. In the next section, you'll read about a concept called "healthism" that reinforces this learning.

SECTION 3
Self-Care

CHAPTER 6
Eating Well

I n this section we're going to look in more detail at HAES from a behavior perspective, starting with food.

Nutrition is a very broad field, encompassing not only the science of how the body uses food (including its relationship to health and disease), but also the implications of food production, manufacturing, and eating. But for those of you who don't want to spend hours studying the ins and outs of biochemistry and global food production, this is your lucky day. We've put together a crash course on nutrition and eating designed to help you grasp enough of the basics to improve your personal health and well-being. (If you do find yourself craving more detailed nutrition information, look for our next book, tentatively titled *Eat Well: For Your Self, for the World*, for a more in-depth discussion, including broader issues such as food politics and the ecological impact of food choices. There's a lot more nuance than we have room for here, and people with specific food intolerances, allergies, sensitivities, or other concerns will need to tailor the recommendations to their needs.)

The Biology of Eating

Let's start with the basic truth about nutrition: We humans need food to survive. To take care of this fundamental need, we come pre-wired with a biological drive to eat. Sensations of hunger and fullness help us nourish and sustain ourselves, and our appetite helps to ensure that a variety of nutrient needs are met. Our body is so invested in getting us to satisfy these needs that not only does it make experiencing excessive hunger and fullness unpleasant, but it rewards us when we do eat, triggering pleasure centers in our brain and making eating that much more enticing. When we have eaten enough to satisfy our energy needs, our bodies actually desensitize our taste receptors so that food doesn't continue to taste as good, encouraging us to stop when we've had enough (providing we respond to these hunger signals and don't override them because we're distracted, bored, etc.).

> Hunger, fullness, appetite, and enjoyment signals provide a much more accurate monitor of your caloric and nutrient needs than calorie counting—and better support health and healthy weight regulation.

You've already learned that because you come packaged with all the information and signals to eat well, you can lighten up on control and let these body signals guide you. What this means is that most of the time, you'll eat when you're hungry and you'll stop when you're full. And you'll also try to eat what you're hungry for and really taste and enjoy your food.

The system isn't foolproof, though. Sometimes you'll fall short of satisfying hunger, and sometimes you'll overshoot "comfortably full." But don't fret; if you can retune your attention to listen to your body signals and trust that they are the best determinants of what you need, you'll be able to intuitively adjust. How cool is that? Rather than having to count calories or try out the latest diet gimmick, all you have to do to get the nutrients you really need is to focus in on what your body is telling you.

We'll also reiterate that eating isn't just about nutrients. Remember our offbeat suggestion that food and eating also fulfill a range of emotional, cultural, and social needs and roles. Approaching food in this way supports an understanding of health as multifaceted and relational—covering social, physical, mental, cultural, and spiritual dimensions of our lives.

In fact, allowing for these roles, and using your body signals, puts you on the best track to match your nutritional requirements. Hunger, fullness, appetite, and enjoyment signals provide a much more accurate monitor of your caloric and nutrient needs than calorie counting—and better support health and healthy weight regulation. There is even research suggesting that guilt messes with your metabolism and weight-regulation system, but enjoyment doesn't; women who felt guilty eating chocolate cake gained weight, while women who viewed it as celebration were more likely to stay weight stable over time.[1] So bust out the balloons and noisemakers and dig into that slice of cake—if you want to. Contrary to popular belief, enjoying your food is actually better for you than guilt-tripping. That's cause for celebration in and of itself!

> Women who felt guilty eating chocolate cake
> gained weight, while women who viewed it as
> celebration were more likely to stay weight sta-
> ble over time.

Energy-Producing Nutrients:
Carbohydrates, Fats, and Proteins

Food not only tastes great—it's also packed with tons of substances that enable our bodies to keep on going. Some of these
substances are more necessary than others for bodily functioning and are classically considered to be "nutrients," such as
carbohydrates, proteins, fats, vitamins, minerals, and, in some
classification systems, water. One of the main reasons we need
nutrients is because some supply us with *energy*. Of course, we
need more than just energy from our food. We also need nutrients that are *building blocks* for making and maintaining cells,
and for making compounds such as hormones, antibodies, and
enzymes. Other nutrients help to *regulate body functions*, and
without them, our health will be compromised.

As you know, not all food is created equal. Though all food
contains energy, the nutrient content of food varies widely. Some
foods are truly superstars from a nutrient perspective, and come
with extra nutritional benefits such as phytochemicals, vitamins, minerals, essential amino acids, essential fatty acids, or
fiber—all of which support our survival and good health. These
VIPs of the food world are known as "nutrient-dense" foods
and supply a lot of beneficial nutrients relative to their energy
content. On the other end of the food-nutrient spectrum are

those known as "energy-dense" foods, which offer a lot of energy relative to their supply of other beneficial nutrients, a trait that may not be so desirable, though they may be superstars from taste or cultural perspectives.

Whether nutrient dense or energy dense, all foods provide energy when the components known as macronutrients are digested and absorbed into our bodies. Don't be put off by their fancy name; macronutrients are none other than carbohydrates, fats, and proteins, which you're most likely already familiar with. Let's take a few moments to review some specific ways the macronutrients affect how we feel. This general information can be useful in helping you anticipate how your food choices will make you feel. The science is not a replacement for your embodied knowledge; it's more of a pointer as you learn what's true for you. Think of learning to eat intuitively like learning to play an instrument. Some folks can tune in straight away and have no need for music scores—they can respond to the instrument effortlessly to get the effect they want. Others appreciate the guidance of a music score until they internalize this knowledge and can dispense with the score and let their fingers and instrument work in harmony.

Carbohydrates

Carbohydrates come in two forms: simple (sugars) or complex (starch and fiber). Foods that contain simple carbohydrates include sugar, sweets, fruits, and dairy products; foods that contain starches include vegetables, beans, and grains; and food sources of fiber include fruits, vegetables, grains, beans, and nuts and seeds when in their whole form. (Processing often damages or removes the fiber.)

Starch is simply a chain of sugar molecules. The digestive process breaks starch down into its component sugars. Your body absorbs those sugars, and they enter your bloodstream. The sugars then circulate around your body, entering cells for use or storage. Despite its bad reputation, sugar is a valuable source of energy for your body.

Foods high in carbohydrates that are quickly digested and absorbed spike your blood sugar levels, followed by a corresponding spike in insulin levels, and as a rule of thumb are less health enhancing (in most situations). In general, simple sugars, refined grains (such as in many cereals and breads), and liquids (such as juiced products) get into your bloodstream quickly, especially when eaten in large quantities or without other foods. Smaller quantities, though they still enter your bloodstream quickly, have little impact on blood sugar and insulin.

Despite its bad reputation, sugar is a valuable source of energy for your body.

In contrast to this fast-track absorption of most simple sugars, the sugars in plant foods, which are less processed and closer to their whole form, trickle into your bloodstream, in part because they are accompanied by fiber. Meals that incorporate some fiber, protein, or fat slow digestion and absorption of carbohydrates, thus decreasing the speed at which the sugar gets into your bloodstream, delivering it at a rate that better matches what your body actually needs and that doesn't flood the system with an overload of sugar and insulin.

Fiber is great for our health in many ways. In addition to slowing the digestion and absorption of sugar, it also helps keep your digestive tract running smoothly. A high-fiber diet reduces the risks for many digestive disorders, as well as for cancer, atherosclerosis, and diabetes.

Many carbohydrate foods (including vegetables, beans, fruits, and whole grains) belong to the category of nutrient-dense foods that we described earlier. They come packaged with other health-enhancing and disease-fighting nutrients, such as vitamins, minerals, and phytochemicals. Others, such as candy or soda, are members of the energy-dense class of foods, and provide you with plenty of energy but few other nutritional benefits.

Sugars don't just affect our digestive health. Sugars on your teeth—which can come from dietary sugar or the starch broken down into sugars by your saliva—feed bacteria, which then release an acid that causes tooth decay. This doesn't mean that you have to avoid carbs. The solution is good dental hygiene— brushing your teeth, flossing, and seeing the dentist regularly. After you drink that juice or soda, swirl a little water around in your mouth to rinse it off your teeth.

APPLICATION FOR HIGH-CARB FOODS

So, in what ways can you mindfully put this knowledge about carbohydrates and the body into practice? Fortunately, it's easier than you may think. You don't need to memorize glycemic index charts that measure how quickly carbohydrates get into the average person's bloodstream, nor do you need to count your carbohydrate grams. Just pay attention to how you feel!

What you'll find is that under ordinary situations, filling up on carbohydrate foods that have greater nutrient density and enter your bloodstream slowly is going to give you more get-up-and-go energy than trying to satisfy your hunger on refined, low-fiber carbs. Practically speaking, this means a shift to increasing intake of vegetables, beans, fruits, and whole grains, and decreasing consumption of simple sugars (except whole fruits) and refined grains. Did you notice that eating smaller quantities at a given time, rather than large meals, also helps your energy levels? This is because small quantities don't spike your blood sugar levels. Including foods that contain fiber, protein, or fat in carbohydrate-rich meals has the same effect, as the combination slows the rise in blood sugar caused by sugars and starches.

In addition to its great role in slowing the digestion and absorption of sugars and starches, fiber will help you to have comfortable bowel movements. In U.S. bathrooms, you'll commonly find magazines. That's a result of the low fiber in North American diets. If constipation is a problem for you, that's your body's way of telling you to up the fiber.

You may be wondering how to start the shift to eating mindfully while also trying to incorporate this information about carbohydrates. Here's something to chew over. Suppose you don't eat many vegetables or whole-grain foods at the moment and want to see if increasing your intake really does give you the boost we've talked about. The trick is to trust the process by checking in with how you feel, both physically and emotionally, as you gradually make small changes in what you eat. Play around a bit with food choices; see what you think and how it feels. Consider, for example, substituting brown rice for white, or buying a vegetable at the farmers' market that you've never eaten and cooking it up. (Ask the purveyor for a favorite recipe!) You may not love everything you try, but you may discover some surprising truths about foods, how they taste, and how they make you feel. The changes will also introduce more variety and new textures, colors, and flavors to your meals, and likely mean you're paying more attention to food choices, and so allocating more time or effort to looking after yourself. These subtle shifts all enrich the role of food and eating. And it doesn't mean you need to fall back into the default position of feeling like a failure if you don't manage to make the choices you hoped to. Just notice what's going on for you. This curious, open-minded awareness actually helps you to get a new angle on the links between your eating, emotions, and experiences—it's all learning. There are no rules, no tables to learn, nothing to fail at, no one judging you. You can think of it as gentle nutrition, or "tasty eating for the curious."

Having said that, we also know that a little knowledge can be a dangerous thing. Talking about the impact of sugar in the body, for example, may cause alarm bells to go off—but consciously setting out to avoid all sugar leads us right back to cognitive restraint and disrupts effortless eating. There are reasons why we may turn to sugary food. We may be seeking an energy boost, we may want a feeling of comfort or control from eating once "forbidden" foods, or it might simply be just what we feel like eating. So, even though we said lots of sugar can flood the system, you don't need to worry if it's what you're reaching for. When you start to legitimize foods and find additional ways of meeting emotional needs without food, you'll probably find that the urge to eat sugary foods diminishes. (That's what both of us have found in our research, and what others have reported as well.) Similarly, once you start tuning in and upping your intake of nutrient-dense carbs, you're not going to need the same quick fixes as you did before, so your overall intake of added sugar will automatically fall. Given the chance, our body supports us in getting more pleasure out of less sugar.

Want to experiment? Taste a sugary food you love—let's say chocolate, as an example. First, try a small bite, let it melt in your mouth, and notice all the sensations. Wait a few seconds, take another bite, and again, be mindful of all the sensations. Now repeat several times. Did you notice the taste buzz diminished over time, and that the later tastes aren't nearly as delicious as the first few? That's a result of your taste buds toning down, a natural physiologic response to support you in noticing when your body's needs have been met. So if you eat foods when they are maximally delicious, you'll find this supports you in eating in a way that doesn't spike your blood sugar. Eat mindfully, enjoy more—that's not a bad deal.

Proteins

Food sources of protein include animal foods such as meat, poultry, fish, eggs, and dairy; and plant foods such as nuts, seeds, beans, grains, and vegetables. In fact, all whole foods contain protein, making it hard to avoid. The only exception is fruit, which contains only a negligible amount.

Eating protein foods along with carbohydrate foods slows the release of sugar into the bloodstream. And protein is also valuable for growth and repair of body tissues. Yet you don't need much, and research shows that most people who get sufficient calories get sufficient protein. Excess protein, which is common in industrialized countries, challenges your health and is associated with increased risk for many diseases, including diabetes, cardiovascular disease, cancer, and kidney disease. So what's helpful to know about protein foods in the body and for health is that there is no nutritional need to build a meal around a concentrated protein source. Unless your diet consists mainly of candy or fruit, you get sufficient protein effortlessly.

Unless your diet consists mainly of candy or fruit, you get sufficient protein effortlessly.

APPLICATION FOR PROTEIN-RICH FOODS

So, how can you mindfully put this knowledge about proteins and the body into practice? If you suspect there could be ways to make your diet work better for you, and you like meat, fish, cheese, and so on, you might want to try moving toward more meals where they are the accompaniment to the plant food centerpiece, and then afterward, notice the change in how you feel. Do you have more or less energy after adding all those veggies? Does it alter when you next feel hungry? How about any effect on bloatedness? These sorts of meals open up some really interesting taste synergies, too. That said, if your absolute favorite meal is steak and fries, enjoy it! We're not talking about a rigid prescription; the aim is to equip you with knowledge about nutrition to inform an exploration of eating differently. Maybe the change starts to alter how you want to present meals, how much variety you look for in flavor, color, and textures in a meal. As a modern-day Ponce de León at the dinner table, you get to bravely explore new foods, applying what you now know to support you in enjoying eating and feeling at your best. You're using your head to initiate the journey, but it's your body that intuitively navigates your course.

Fats

Poor fats. They have to be the most vilified of all the food groups, blamed for a host of health problems and shunned by people seeking to improve their health or lose weight. Contrary to popularized messages, however, fats serve important functions in our body, and a fat-free diet is not a healthy diet—nor does it prove to be any more successful in accomplishing sustained weight loss. Believe it or not, there is no convincing evidence that a low-fat diet is beneficial for the majority of individuals. It's more the type of fat—not the overall amount of fat—that is important to health.

What's helpful to know about fatty foods in the body and for health? Fats are an important source of energy and nutrients; they taste delicious, smell enticing, and add texture in foods and cooking.

> There is no convincing evidence that a low-fat diet is beneficial for the majority of individuals.

The table shows main food sources of the different fats. Bear in mind that it's an approximation; nature doesn't neatly compartmentalize things to fit nutrition categories! Some meats contain significant amounts of monounsaturated fats, for instance.

MAIN FOOD SOURCES OF THE DIFFERENT FATS				
Saturated	Mono-unsaturated	Poly-unsaturated (omega-3)	Poly-unsaturated (not omega-3)	Trans Fats
Butter	Olive oil	Oily fish	Vegetable oils (most)	Processed foods (some)*
Lard	Canola (rapeseed) oil	Flaxseed		Deep-fried foods (some)
Meat		Hemp		*Look for "partially hydrogenated" in the ingredients.
Poultry	Avocados	Walnuts		
Dairy products	Nuts (most)	Soy products		
Coconut oil		Foods from grass-fed animals		

APPLICATION FOR FATTY FOODS

If you've trained yourself to eat low fat, now's the time to rethink that decision. If your motivation was weight control, legitimizing foods—that is, giving yourself permission to eat what you want when you want, and being guided along the way by tuning in to body signals—really is the best way to arrive at a weight that's healthy for you. If general health was the primary driver, then rest assured that you need fats for well-being, and a low-fat diet is not necessarily a healthier diet. The fact that many of us don't consume enough of some types of fats is what we really need to address. A common nutritional imbalance is a low intake of omega-3 fats and a skewed ratio of omega-3s to omega-6s in the diet. This imbalance is not hard to correct; try cooking with canola (rapeseed) rather than corn oil, for example, and having oily fish or meat from grass-fed animals, or plant sources of an omega-3 precursor (a substance that "goes before," i.e., gets converted to omega-3) such as flaxseeds. Meanwhile, if you're tucking into more beans, whole grains, and vegetables, then you'll gradually be reducing your intake of the trans fats found in processed foods—a helpful health bonus—anyway. And you'll similarly be reducing your intake of saturated fats by shifting away from an animal foods–based diet, which may also improve your health profile. (The jury is out on the health effects of saturated fats; high levels are associated with increased disease risk, although it's hard to isolate the effects of saturated fats from those of the other nutrients they are often packaged with. Moderate intake doesn't appear to be problematic.) If you start loosening up a bit around fats as you explore new food choices, you may be pleasantly surprised by how liberated you feel.

Non-Energy-Producing Nutrients: The Micronutrients

Now that we've covered the basics about macronutrients, let's turn to substances known as micronutrients, including vitamins, minerals, and phytochemicals. As the name suggests, we need smaller amounts of these compounds to maintain good health, but a little goes a long way! These are important features of a diet that is going to nourish us.

Vitamins

A vitamin is an organic compound (meaning, in this usage, that it contains carbon) that your body requires to regulate functions within cells. Vitamins affect a wide variety of functions in your body, such as promoting good vision, forming healthy blood cells, creating strong bones and teeth, and ensuring good performance of your heart and nervous system. While they don't supply energy, some of them help you extract the energy from macronutrients.

Minerals

Minerals come from the earth, and in contrast to vitamins, they are inorganic (don't contain carbon). They are absorbed into water and taken up by plants through water or soil, and are transferred to animals that consume the mineral-laden plants and water. Humans get minerals through drinking water or eating plants or animals that contain them. Minerals help with many vital body functions, such as bone formation or effective functioning of the nervous and digestive systems and the heart.

It's interesting to note that the most common mineral recommendation is to reduce the amount of sodium in our diets by cutting down on salt—yet scientific solidity for the low-salt message is in dispute.[2] A stronger argument can be made that sodium reduction may only be beneficial in the context of other dietary changes, and only for some individuals.[3] For the general population salt intake plays a minor role in blood pressure regulation and does not appear to be a determinant of cardiovascular disease outcomes, quality of life, or longevity.

Phytochemicals

A phytochemical is a health-promoting compound found in plants that is not a vitamin, mineral, or macronutrient. Though phytochemicals promote good health, they are not essential for life. Phytochemicals protect plants against the elements, and confer these benefits on us when we eat them. For example, sulforaphane glucosinolates (try saying that one three times fast!) found in broccoli protect against macular degeneration, high blood pressure, and several cancers. And the resveratrol found in ginger and grapes (and yes, wine) can help combat cancer.

Micronutrients

To get the biggest nutrient investment when you eat, include nutrient-dense foods you enjoy. The following list approximately ranks foods in order of their nutrient density; a useful strategy is to maximize consumption of foods that appear earlier in the list:

Vegetables

Beans

Fruits

Whole grains

Nuts and seeds

Fish, meat, and dairy

Processed foods

As you experiment with more plant foods and new combinations for meals, you'll also get a feast for your eyes and palate. Eating a wide variety of foods will help ensure that you get the variety and amounts of micronutrients that you need, and you won't need to tote up your intake on any charts.

Water

Water is essential to body functioning—even getting rid of it is good for you, by flushing out contaminants and preventing mineral deposits. Among its many functions, water:

- Acts as a medium for chemical reactions to occur
- Helps regulate body temperature
- Fills cells and the space between them, and acts as a lubricant
- As a major portion of blood and urine, helps to carry nutrients to cells and remove waste
- Aids digestion and the movement of nutrients through your gastrointestinal tract

Thirst is an indication of low hydration and that your body is not functioning optimally, so it's best to drink in advance of thirst. This is one instance when body knowledge can be a bit slow off the mark, and a good time to let our brains take the helm for once instead of following the lead of our bodily sensations. Most people don't drink enough water and so would feel better—more alert, better digestion—if they drank more. How do you know if you're well hydrated? First, try drinking a bit more during the day and notice if you feel differently (i.e., better). Also, clear or light-colored urine is a sign of good hydration, while yellow urine is often a sign of dehydration. (Sometimes substances in foods can confuse you, however. High quantities of vitamin C or B-complex, for example, will make your urine yellow even if you are well hydrated. And have you ever been victim to the post-beet, or post-beetroot, scare, when your urine takes on a bloody tint?)

Beyond Nutrients

Now that we've covered the many health-promoting powers of micronutrients and macronutrients, we must introduce one other possible component of foods, the "anti-nutrients." As the name suggests, these are the pitfalls of nutrition, which serve to weaken our well-being and health. These include substances such as pesticides and residues from plastics and other pollutants. These anti-nutrients also impact our health (and weight). The easiest rule of thumb is: the fewer additives and modifications, the better. We're big supporters of food grown with attention to sustainability and respect toward the people who grow the food, other animals, and ecology. But that's another book. (Look for it soon: *Eat Well: For Your Self, for the World!*)

Putting It All Together

How can someone concerned about health make sense of the debate about whether to eat high carbohydrate, high protein, or high fat? Just how many portions of fruit and veggies do you really need to thrive? The research regarding the basics of healthy nutrition hasn't really changed in the past century. The challenge we face now is how to help people unlearn dieting and pursue mindful eating. Paying attention to how your food choices influence your physical well-being and moods will lead you toward choosing a more nutritious diet, and one that works for you. The best nutritionist you know lies within your skin. If you're mindful of body signals, you'll find, for example, that you function best with plenty of fiber, so you don't need to follow some external rule about fiber consumption. You'll find out how you feel if you regularly have meals low in carbs, or start drinking water more regularly. Your body really does know best when it comes to getting what it needs to sustain itself; your job is to listen carefully and respectfully and to trust what you feel.

The best nutritionist you know lies within your skin.

Feel drawn to foods that aren't optimal for your health? As we pointed out with sugary foods, the first step to responding to these drives may surprise you. Let yourself eat them! Like most "forbidden fruits," eating something that's allowable isn't nearly as tempting as eating something deemed off-limits. The research shows that both children and adults actually eat less "junk" food when it's permitted—and that this "off-limit" approach to parental restriction of food backfires in the long run.

If you do find yourself caught in the bind of craving foods you think you'd feel better eating less of, rest assured that you're not destined for a lifetime of fighting the urge. Instead, you can actually change your preferences and tastes over time. For example, your taste buds, and many other sensory cells, constantly regenerate. If you don't use all your sugar receptors for a few weeks, they don't regenerate in the same quantity. Then, when you go back to high-sugar foods, they taste sickeningly sweet and less appealing. Foods that are less sweet become more appealing to you. In other words, if you reduce your sugar habit for a bit, you may find it becomes a natural choice in the long run and that high quantities of overly sweet stuff no longer have the same appeal—you don't have to fight the urge to reach for them, because there isn't one!

Despite the message of just about every diet plan out there, the path to healthy nutrition is not paved with rigid rules and guilt. They won't help you make better choices in the long run. Flexibility will serve you well and sustain your long-term pursuit of better health; there is plenty of room for less nutrient-dense choices in a diet that nourishes you. Honoring the pleasure in eating will help you stay satisfied and on track to effortless eating. Also, you can trust that your body is pretty good about making up for those "delicious beyond fullness" decisions when you follow a general pattern of respecting its signals.

So for anyone interested in a "how-to" of getting started with mindful eating, here's the advice in a nutshell: Honor your body and eat only delicious food. Tune in to hunger and see how it goes when you go to the table hungry but not famished, enjoy your food, and eat until you are satisfied. If emotions arise around your food choices, be gentle with yourself as you acknowledge them. Try to intentionally savor and appreciate what you eat. As you're attentive to the effect that food has on you, you'll learn to let this increasingly intuitive knowledge guide your choices.

In time, being attentive to the effect food has on you may lead you more toward basing your diet on whole (unprocessed or minimally processed) foods. If you make sure you get plenty of variety, you'll be getting all the nutrients you need, and, of foods that are less nutrient dense and mainly meet other, non-nutritional roles, you'll still be eating what satisfies you.

The Challenge of Eating Well in an Eating-Disordered Culture

Trusting Your Body to Guide Eating

What would it be like to not have to think about weight control or what you eat? Infants are great examples of this principle:

They eat when they're hungry—only what they want—and stop when they're satisfied. Research shows that when young children are given a wide variety of foods and free rein to choose what they want, they instinctively choose a diet containing appropriate energy.[3] On the other hand, restriction fosters consumption in the absence of physical hunger and, conversely, pressuring children to eat "healthy food" is counterproductive, turning them off to those foods.[4]

This skill to eat mindfully and make nourishing choices is innate and within all of us, once we drop the external rules, as Linda, Lucy, and others have demonstrated in their research.

Research shows that when young children are given a wide variety of foods and free rein to choose what they want, they instinctively choose a diet containing appropriate energy.

Within our cultural context it's hard not to feel uncomfortable with eating. Because dieting has become a national pastime, the pain it causes and reflects can easily pass unnoticed. But it's not obligatory to hate our bodies or fear food. Unhelpful ideas about what our bodies are supposed to look like, and what and how much we're supposed to eat to achieve that, result in disconnection from our bodies and distrust of our body's needs around food—and can lead to disordered eating habits. Many of us come to believe that our body signals need to be ignored and our desires controlled.

Disordered Eating as a Cultural Response

> Several women were sitting in a campus dining room talking about eating disorders. One woman casually commented: "Oh, I wouldn't mind getting anorexia. I could be happy getting rid of these saddlebags!" The other women laughed in agreement.

Dieting Disorders

The desire to change one's weight is a fairly common denominator in the etiology (cause) of eating disorders, so they could perhaps more appropriately be called "dieting disorders."* The consequences are more than cosmetic. In fact, eating disorders compromise quality of life for many people, and are sometimes even life threatening. Unfortunately, they often don't elicit the cultural concern that is warranted, as demonstrated by the preceding conversation among the college women that Linda overheard in a campus dining room. We need to be talking more seriously about these disorders, and we need to be concerned about the cultural attitudes and public "health" messages that encourage them.

You don't need an eating disorder diagnosis to feel the distress associated with disordered eating. Consider the following:

- ▨ Are you excessively concerned about your body size, and the impact of the food you eat on your weight?
- ▨ Do you feel guilty or ashamed of your eating habits?
- ▨ Do you strictly avoid certain foods because you believe they are fattening?

---

* The term "dieting disorders" was coined by psychologist Dr. Deb Burgard.

■ Do you use laxatives or diuretics, make yourself vomit, or exercise excessively in an effort to manage your weight?

Wherever you fit on the spectrum, if you feel uncomfortable—label or not—start talking about it and reaching out for help. We give you strategies in Chapter 8 to handle a very common behavior, often called "emotional eating," and encourage those of you struggling with these concerns to seek help beyond this book. Be sure to query whether the "expert" you turn to comes from a Health at Every Size perspective; some in the eating disorders field still approach weight as a problem to be solved and dieting as positive self-care. Check out the free database of practitioners and clinics in the HAES community resource listings at www.HAESCommunity.org.

Body Insecurity

If you're caught in the throes of body insecurity—and believe that controlling your diet will get you out of that mess—there are good reasons why you got there. We all experience enormous pressure to conform to unrealistic cultural standards of beauty and what health is supposed to look like. This takes place in a context that presumes that controlling eating can help you effectively achieve that body ideal, a myth we've thoroughly deconstructed earlier in this book.

Advertising for many commercial goods functions by cultivating our body insecurity or hatred in order to sell products. If we all believed we were attractive as we are, for example, we would have little need for most commercial beauty products. Women in particular are taught that their self-worth is determined by how well they match the cultural standard of beauty.

Most of us therefore feel inadequate and that we can never measure up. And it seems as if advertisers have recently realized that they were so busy exploiting women's insecurities, they'd forgotten half the population. So now they're doing their best to make men feel equally horrible about themselves. Buying into these images doesn't benefit anyone but the advertisers.

Advertisers have recently realized that they were so busy exploiting women's insecurities, that they'd forgotten half the population. So now they're doing their best to make men feel equally horrible about themselves.

Worse, while advertising contributes to body hatred, the authority granted to anti-fat messages in medicine and science reinforces the message, making health campaigns a health hazard.

While it is hard to survive the cultural and medical onslaught, not everyone develops eating distress or an eating disorder. The key issue that distinguishes those who do from those who don't—or establishes where they are on the continuum—is their degree of self-esteem. Self-esteem refers to how you feel about yourself and is strongly influenced by your life experiences and support. If you have high self-esteem, you value who you are, as you are. The lower your self-esteem, the more you measure yourself against an outside standard—a standard you can never meet—with painful ramifications. Besides our own feelings about our self-worth, genetic propensity also plays a role in the development of eating disorders.

We're going to mention one pattern of eating distress in more detail because it is particularly insidious and may pass unrecognized, as its victims, tolerantly called "health food junkies," are often applauded for what can be a dangerous obsession. "Orthorexia nervosa" refers to an obsessive concern with the health content of food. Do you wish that you could just enjoy eating and not worry about its health implications? While many people experience this discomfort to some degree, it turns into orthorexia when it limits your ability to develop relationships and other interests.

Orthorexia is not a current clinical diagnosis, and its place as a bona fide eating disorder is being debated among health care professionals. Regardless of whether it meets the classic criteria for an eating disorder, a rigid fixation on "eating right" can be just as painful as any other eating disorder. It also illustrates what happens when as a society we encourage people to pursue their personal health as the be-all and end-all. People can be supported in orthorexic habits because of social mores that endorse their restrictive eating as something to which we should all aspire. In this, it illustrates the concept of healthism.

Healthism would have us eat this, or move more, not because it's fun and we feel better for it and want to enjoy the day, but because of a civic, at times grim, duty to be healthy. Healthist thinking makes the mistake of reducing health to the sum of our health behaviors, and leads people to overlook vital factors such as relationships, oppression, humor, love, and world peace that significantly impact health outcomes and give our lives meaning. It also suggests that the pursuit of personal health should be our highest ambition. This creates a culture where people are shamed and judged according to how closely they accept and meet this belief, and spawns a health care environment where it becomes normal for people to be patronized, cajoled, coerced, and bullied into following advice. If you'd like to enjoy eating and not worry about its health implications, or read what's in your cupboard as a statement on your own or someone else's character, try dropping the harsh, black-and-white, individual-istic thinking of healthism for the more rounded, inclusive, and compassionate approach of HAES.

CHAPTER 7
Enthused to Move

My [Linda's] palms were sweaty, my heart was racing, and my head was running through the excuses I could use to turn back. I was trying to get up the courage to join my partner for our first salsa dancing class. I got dealt two left feet when it comes to grace and ears that can't find a beat, so dancing has never been my forte. Yet I'd always been jealous watching dancers; dancing seems like such a fun and romantic way to be together. An hour later I left, a sweaty mess with a big smile on my face, feeling all full of love and the joy of connection.

Exercise doesn't have to be a "workout." It can be fun, energizing, and oh, so much more. We don't have to convince you of its benefits; you already know it's great stuff. In fact, why don't you tell us? Time yourself for two minutes and see how many benefits of being active/exercising you can come up with.

Active Living

There's no doubt that physical activity is toward the top of the list of lifestyle habits that influence your health. Physical activity or, to put it more simply, movement triggers tremendous changes in your musculoskeletal and cardiovascular systems and in the hormones and neurotransmitters involved in health, such as the all-important relaxation response. It also impacts pathways involved in weight regulation; activity even helps you become more sensitive to hunger and satiety signals.

Exercise doesn't have to be a "workout." It can be fun, energizing, and oh, so much more.

Lots of people are temporarily motivated to become more active because they want to lose weight. While exercise is very important to health, it's not likely to lead to long-term weight loss. The failure of physical activity to achieve this end results in people becoming demotivated to be active, together with feelings of being a failure, guilt, and disillusion: All that effort and for what? It also means we're back in the confines of the energy balance equation, where exercise is understood as "good for you" because of its connection to weight loss. The many other benefits of being active—all those you just came up with on your list—can get lost in the focus on weight management. Even if we take weight out of the equation, approaching activity as something you "should" do because it's "good for you" and you feel the pressure to be healthy is also a limited way of looking at things that has us back meeting external goals rather than listening to, and enjoying, our bodies.

The projected weight impact doesn't motivate most people to *stay* active. People who exercise regularly tend to do so because it gives them an enormous sense of well-being. They feel more energetic throughout the day, sleep better at night, have sharper memories and clearer minds, and feel more relaxed and positive about themselves and their lives. And it doesn't take hours of pumping weights in a gym or running mile after mile to achieve those results.

When we switch our focus to finding ways of being active that make us feel good and that we can fit into our schedules, we're on the road to living life more fully.

Instead, we can approach activity with the expectation of having fun and feeling better for the time spent moving our bodies, maybe in the company of friends or with a class or team we're glad to belong to. This takes away the sense of grim obligation many adults associate with activity. When we switch our focus to finding ways of being active that make us feel good and that we can fit into our schedules, we're on the road to living life more fully.

This new approach requires that we let go of judging ourselves according to the amount of exercise we've done, or how hard we worked at it. Instead of feeling bad for only walking for thirty-five minutes when we told ourselves we'd definitely do an hour, we accept that thirty-five minutes was the best we could manage when it came down to it, which unclips us from the emotionally draining cycle of self-blame and frees us to appreciate what we did and get on with our day. When we take the judgment out and learn to tune in to our bodies, we'll find ways to move, stretch, relax, strengthen, and push our bodies that optimize our feelings of well-being.

Under this framework, the aim is to tune in to our bodies to enjoy a range of activities that optimize our day-to-day sense of vitality and support our overall mental, physical, and social well-being. The research shows that switching focus to pleasurable movement (play!), health gain, and body attunement is far more effective in supporting a sustained increase in activity level than a focus on exercise for weight loss. You'll notice this definition of what we can think of as "realistic fitness" applies equally well to someone with limited mobility as it does to an elite athlete.

What Stops You?

Here are some common responses to what holds people back:

You say: "I don't have enough time to exercise."

We say: Even short intervals of movement can act as a powerful tool to supercharge your health. Climb a flight of stairs if you're physically able; it will lift your mood as well as your body—and often takes less time than waiting for an elevator.

You say: "Exercise is too difficult and painful."

We say: "No pain, no gain" is so old school. Exercise doesn't have to hurt to be incredibly effective. You don't have to push yourself to the limit to get results. Even cleaning the house with a bit of vigor will give you a boost.

You say: "I'm too tired to exercise."

We say: Movement is a powerful pick-me-up that can significantly reduce fatigue and make you feel much more energetic. Try it next time you're tired. See what happens.

You say: "I'm too ungainly/lazy/fat/skinny/daunted/stiff/old . . ."

We say: It's never too late to start building your strength, flexibility, and physical fitness, even if you're a senior or a couch potato who has never exercised before. We've heard countless people say they are lazy—the same folks who have made extraordinary efforts to lose weight. That amount of effort is not laziness! Or maybe you're somebody for whom "lazy" has come to mean, "I spend so much time looking after others I forget I need time for me, too."

You say: "I'm too unfit!"

We say: No one gets written off. Experiment until you find the right activities for *your* body. Get advice if you have health problems or specific needs; get moral support from friends to take the first step—which might be to soak up the daylight from your open door before walking to the gate.

You say: "Exercise is boring."

We say: Sure, pounding on a treadmill may not be everyone's idea of a good time. But not everything that raises our heart rate or gets us stretching has to be boring. Ask a gardening enthusiast! When you say, "But I don't like exercising," what you're really saying is, "I don't enjoy the particular type of exercise that I have in mind." Expand your horizons. We've got plenty of ideas below to get you thinking. When you do find something that works for you, notice how you feel afterward. Sensing and recalling that buzz will help rewrite your memory to, "I feel great when I get out and . . ."

Not Exercise, but "What I'm Doing"

Now that we've got the major gremlins out of the way, let's discuss this new framing.

If you think hitting the gym or sprinting around the block is required but it's not your bag, don't stress. Routine activities such as vacuuming the living room can be as beneficial as strenuous aerobic exercise, or more so for some people. This is part of a new model for exercise called "active living." Active living refers to moving more as part of your everyday life. It means taking the stairs instead of the elevator; raking the leaves yourself instead of recruiting a neighborhood child to do it or using a leaf blower; or parking at a distant spot instead of circling the parking lot looking for the closest space.

Some people love the exercise-class culture and team-sport scene. But for those of us not so inclined, know that there's evidence that people who shift their focus to active living are maintaining these activity patterns for up to two years or more, which is in direct contrast to the short-lived attempts of people who jump on the gym bandwagon.[1]

So forget about carving time out for your workout, if that's not appealing to you. Instead, just find ways to integrate more movement into your daily life. To be most successful, keep it simple and don't ask or expect too much of yourself. Instead, think of creative ways you can move more without making major alterations to your schedule—start where you are. Look for the feel-good factor: The point is to find ways to appreciate and enjoy your body, to feel revitalized, and maybe also to heal any mind-body disconnect. It is not about any obligation to "be healthy" or "burn calories." We've suggested a list from our own experience, but you can come up with ideas that suit your life and abilities:

- Wear or keep comfortable walking shoes in the office or car. Any time you have to wait or have a few minutes to spare, take a walk.
- Park far from your destination and walk to it.
- Walk to a different floor or neighboring building to use the restroom.
- Deliver things personally instead of using interoffice mail or email.
- Stand, stretch, and move every waking hour.
- Walk around when talking on the phone.
- Hold walking meetings instead of sitting in an office.
- Set challenges for yourself: If the stairs aren't busy, can you time yourself between floors?
- Play a childhood game. Tag? Capture the flag? Kick the can? Get some friends together and relive the playfulness.
- Meet a friend once a week and shoot some hoops (basketball) while you catch up with each other.
- Use an app or your calendar to remind yourself to take time to be active.

- Walk or cycle to the store instead of driving.

- Get off the bus or subway at an earlier stop.

- Play chase with your dog. Or someone else's dog; their human companion is sure to appreciate it.

- Park at the far end of the mall and window-shop until you reach your destination.

- Go the long way past the park and appreciate the trees, the shade, the birdsong, and the fountain.

- Clean. Make a game of it. Dance with your vacuum. Pump the music up and rock to the beat while folding clothes.

- Roughhouse with your kids. The little ones will also love to dance and get silly with you! Or how about a game of Ping-Pong (or table tennis) or an activity-based video game?

- Throw away the TV remote control.

- Compete with your buddy. Who can find the most outlandish garden display on a walk? Or the most plastic pink flamingos? Text each other pictures of the contenders you find!

- Stand and march in place while reading on the computer. (Easier in the privacy of your own home!)

- Walk with your friends and colleagues instead of taking the usual coffee break.

- Try yoga. There are many versions of yoga, so sign up for a few different kinds and see which one lines up the best with what you're looking for. You can find some classes that are vigorous, others that emphasize slow breathing, others that are heated. . . . In some towns, you can even find classes that are clothing optional.

- Use an old-fashioned push mower for lawn work.

- Go geocaching—it's an adventure nerd's dream come true. Become a real-life treasure hunter and have a great time doing it.

- Explore the outdoors, on foot or bike.

- Take up bird-watching, or get curious about plants and bugs.

- Have more sex. And sex doesn't have to be reserved for partners. Go for it on your own for additional feel-good.

With these activities, challenge yourself by adding them into your life gradually and then increasing the frequency at which you do them. Do small bouts and enjoy the enhanced sense of vitality that comes from moving more. If you climb four flights of stairs one day, add an extra one the next. But don't feel the pressure to push yourself. As you'll find, even a little bit has big payback.

The beauty of this approach is that you can forget about any fitness plan, weight loss, target heart rate, number of calories burned, and so forth. Instead, just move. An added bonus? Just a single short stint of activity will release endorphins, feel-good chemicals that pick up your mood immediately. It also makes muscle cells more responsive to insulin, even when you're not moving, which will help you manage your blood sugar, reducing your risk of diabetes and other conditions. And regular activity will also bump up serotonin production and uptake, contributing to a greater sense of well-being all the time.

Not Physical Activity, but "Minding the Body"

The idea of activity optimizing our everyday well-being also opens dimensions of embodiment that can fall by the wayside in a more traditional approach to physical health. While there is certainly increasing recognition of the value of the mind-body connection in mainstream services, the conventional, instrumental approaches to activity still tend to be primarily concerned with conditioning the body. Focusing on the body means we can miss other aspects of physicality related to mindfulness, the connection between mind and body. There are many activities where what's going on, and what can be offered, cannot be meaningfully measured in terms of calories burned or muscles used. You'll already have spotted some examples of these in the preceding list. Another example: Let's say a person with limited mobility also suffers from chronic pain. As well as any benefit this person may derive from being more active, he or she can pursue strategies for tuning in to his or her body that can help with pain management and sleep. Breathing and relaxation exercises, and some forms of martial arts, can help people manage stress and develop emotional connection and awareness.

It might be more helpful if, instead of thinking about "physical activity," we thought about "minding the body." The idea of minding the body can help us get some distance from thinking of our bodies—and thus ourselves—as machines to keep in working order. It includes physical activity, but it doesn't stop there—it also has room for relaxation and related practices, plus pampering and sensual experiences. Add humor, hugs, and laughter. But we don't need to stop there, either—how about embodiment as self-expression and creativity, such as in singing, performance, and dance? And minding the body allows for emotional, social, and spiritual dimensions in our lives. The experience of, and health benefits from, walking a mile down a busy road are very different from those that result from walking in green spaces. Expanding how we think of our embodiment helps us bring this bigger picture into view and get out of the thinking trap where a one-mile walk amounts to X number of steps and X number of calories burned.

Simply put, in the words of the HAES course, Well Now, *Be your body's buddy!*

CHAPTER 8
Emotional Empowerment

D o you find yourself attacking a pint—or gallon—of ice cream when you're lonely, depressed, or merely bored? Many of us have learned to turn to food to ride out emotions that unsettle us. This is because food can help us manage our emotions. Eating tempers emotion and temporarily gets us back on an even keel, bringing us to a more familiar and comfortable state. This is the case whether the emotions are labeled positive, negative, extreme, or neutral states—be it happiness or anger, excitement or boredom.

We have already circled the topic of emotions and eating in Chapter 6. In this chapter we'll take a closer look at how we can work with our emotions to heal our relationship with food. Some people will be able to use these ideas to transform their eating over time. Other people will benefit from the help of a skilled practitioner to support them through the process.

Emotional Eating

The drive to eat when you are not physically hungry means that you need something—and food is either the stand-in while you figure out what the underlying need is, or the substitute means of meeting that need if it remains unidentified. This is not a time to come down on yourself! When you reach for food at these times it's because it's the best way you know in that moment to take care of yourself. It's a resourceful attempt to manage emotions, and plenty of folks with a healthy relationship with food will comfort-eat from time to time. The problem arises when it's the *only* way you have to manage emotions and it leads to turning to food a lot—every time you feel off-kilter—because then the coping behavior itself causes distress.

Acknowledge that if you are an "emotional eater," your strategy has played a vital role in self-care when you didn't have other options available to you. For example, when I (Linda) was younger and feeling lonely, I didn't have the emotional skills to take care of myself. Eating was very effective at diverting me from the loneliness I felt. It helped me get through tough times, and was generally pretty dependable.

But then my obsession with weight surfaced, and suddenly food wasn't as effective in helping me. Sure, it tempered the feelings in the moment. But this was only a short-lived comfort, followed by a more intense and longer-lasting guilt. The weight I gained served as evidence of my failure and another reason to come down on myself.

This is where most of us get stuck. We recognize the short-term comfort or pleasure we get from food and, without other skills to take care of ourselves in the moment, we depend on it for an instant feel-better fix. But doing so does not mitigate our feelings in the long run, and gives us the added burden of guilt and anger about our eating habits and their ramifications on our weight. In a society intent on judging people, and especially one that is so moralistic around food, health, and weight, it can be hard to move on from this cycle of distress, eating, beating yourself up, and then feeling more distress. Being kind to ourselves is one step we can start practicing right away.

Exploring Your Emotions

Emotional Regulation

What can you do when you feel the drive to eat and you know that you are not physically hungry? Start by acknowledging how important it is to take care of yourself. Without food or another technique, life could be pretty difficult and overwhelming. Show appreciation for the help you have gotten in the past from food. But now, decide that you're going to turn to something else as well to assist you in managing your emotions, examining options that will more fully help you deal with them instead of just holding them at bay.

To learn a new coping mechanism, begin with understanding what you're feeling. Explore your emotions more thoroughly and try to identify what you are really looking for and what it would take to satisfy your need. How does it feel to acknowledge those feelings and address them more directly? If you tell your friend you are angry at her, how does that make you feel? Does that change your drive to eat? Now, what else can you do differently? If you write a letter to her, even if you never intend to give it to her, does that make you feel better? Does it curb your desire to reach for food? If you sound off to a partner about the situation, does that help settle your emotions? If you take a furious walk down the hall, will that be more effective for you than eating? Will watching a funny movie lift your spirits more than digging into a bowl of ice cream? If you bring a book to read while waiting for your appointment, does that seem more fulfilling than the candy bar? Can you find compassion for the friend who let you down—and for your own angry attack in response?

Learning to identify and own our emotions—without judgment, however difficult they may be—is a first step in effectively using them and/or soothing ourselves. Then we can expand the portfolio of choices we make when responding to our emotions so that food is only one of many ways we soothe ourselves, if that's what we need. This means we start to make sense of our eating, which allows us to move on, gently and with compassion for ourselves and others. Identifying and owning an emotion allows it to surface as useful information, and can help us regain a clarity that includes this emotional knowledge, but is not overwhelmed by it. We don't get access to this knowledge if we respond to all emotional upheaval by eating. The eating has certainly met a need—otherwise we wouldn't have done it—but learning to engage more fully with our emotional landscape once it's safe to do so is a more rewarding way to experience the world.

It can also be difficult to access emotional knowledge and other body signals if we've learned to live in our heads, which can happen for many reasons, including in response to early trauma. The body-mind integration that comes with learning to listen to our feelings, body signals, and sensations can be profoundly healing and can help us become more emotionally savvy. Being able to put our emotions and other body wisdom into the mix contributes to self-trust and an enhanced sense of agency.

Remember, the "problem" is not that you're overeating. The problem is that you don't yet have a comfortable way to tolerate your emotional challenges. Learning to accept that all emotions are okay, and to be curious about them and your eating behaviors, will help you better match your actions and your needs. Your emotional eating may decrease—not because of extra self-control, but from becoming your own best friend and exploring new ways to look after your body-self. This means in turn you'll be better able to work out what it is you need, so you'll be better able to take care of yourself. This in itself reduces distressing emotions. Because you have lots of ways to respond, you won't always have to use food as the quick fix for unsettled emotions. So when you do choose food, it really will be comfort eating, not another link in the distress cycle.

The overwhelming drive to eat will dissipate as you develop skills for identifying and meeting your emotional needs, letting go of any judgment. Of course, you may need many times to notice this before your behavior changes, during which food may still be a useful stopgap, so be patient. The sense of being compelled to eat and being out of control with food can also come from simply being too hungry. This panicked eating lessens as you learn to tune in to body cues so you eat earlier, rather than waiting until you are famished.

Accepting Your Body

We've just described how accepting our emotions can help us make sense of our eating as we learn to distinguish between hunger that is mainly emotional and hunger that is mainly physical. There's also a link with body acceptance. We'd be surprised if you haven't had conflicted feelings about accepting your body. Perhaps one day you're feeling great about yourself, and the next day it's a struggle to recapture that same sense of okay-ness. Or maybe the shift is from hour to hour, or happens when you come across something sizeist—a remark, an image, inaccessible furniture.

Here's the thing: Your ambivalence is okay. You're okay. Self-acceptance is rarely available to us as an overnight wonder pill where we wake up unconditionally loving ourselves. In real life, the journey forward is not that smooth, and likely will be punctuated with the trips and stumbles of painful emotions and conflicting positions. What the HAES approach makes newly available to you is the idea that it's okay to be confused, conflicted, contradictory—contrary, even! There's no rule that says you are okay only if you love your body. Everyone deserves respect, and when someone is struggling they can use an extra bit of kindness. As you move away from the black-white trap of the dieting mentality, you'll likely find you are more comfortable with uncertainty than you used to be; this in turn makes it easier to deal with difficult emotions without judging them or getting caught up in them.

We cannot emphasize enough the value in lightening up around the judgment you may feel about your body and your weight. The judgment evokes despair as you believe there is something wrong with you, meaning you are not entitled to the food that you want, and you need to deprive yourself as punishment or remedy for your "overweight."

Accepting Your Appetite

In fact, the severe judgment you cast on yourself can cause a powerful retaliatory appetite. Being judgmental about your appetite or weight or emotions will interfere with intuitive eating because judgment introduces rules of "should" and "ought" that divert you from listening to your body signals. If this happens, you're still okay; accept it as part of your learning process. If difficult emotions surface, simply noticing them in a curious, open-minded way, rather than denying or fighting them, can move us from resistance to acceptance, and acceptance is the cornerstone of transformation. The more comfortable you feel in accepting your appetite, emotions, and body as they are, the less you will feel driven or compelled to eat, and the more you will feel at peace around food and skilled at meeting your needs.

The Bonus of Mindfulness

By now you'll no doubt have picked up on the idea that paying attention to our feelings, thoughts, and ideas, without judgment, can help free us from patterns of beliefs and behaviors that lead to self-defeating habits and make us feel stuck.

Tuning in to our bodies and paying attention to body signals, as with mindful eating and active embodiment, is a step on the way to "mindfulness" practice. Mindfulness is described as paying attention in a particular way:

- On purpose
- In the present moment
- Nonjudgmentally

We can practice mindfulness by setting aside ten minutes or so on a daily basis to quiet the mind and simply notice what's going on in our bodies. There are heaps of free downloads available on the web to guide beginners through different types of mindfulness exercises. These range from scanning the body, to guided meditations, to watching your breath, to visualizations, and more. Over time, practicing mindfulness, and the acceptance (nonjudgment) that goes with it, can enhance our clarity and sense of well-being. Mindfulness practice can also impact our critical-awareness skills and enable us to make better sense of our emotional life and life experiences. Altogether, regular mindfulness practice is very nurturing and helps equip us to ride out the roller coaster of our internal and external worlds.

And if you appreciate a more visual prompt for self-care, you can take the Body Respect Pledge . . . today and every day. Copy it and keep it handy (see page 187).

SECTION 4
Cultivating Body Respect

CHAPTER 9
The Personal Journey

Imagine waking up one day and finding you're at peace with your body and self. It feels good, right? So consider: How does a day that starts like that become different than the day before? Think about the effects in your relationships, work, and social time. One way of moving toward the world we want to live in is to practice living in it now. Can you connect with the feelings and thoughts that go along with this sense of being at peace? What do you need to think or do to conjure them up?

Steps to Building Respect for Your Body

There is no magic formula to heal from body discomfort. It is a personal path, different for everyone.

The first step, however, is universal: Be gentle with yourself. You've been doing your best—there is nothing to be ashamed of, either about your body or for wanting to change it. There will be times when you find yourself yearning to be another size; be gentle with yourself. Maybe you get frustrated that you're not able to just love the body you've got; again, go easy on yourself.

Let compassion and acceptance lead the way. The next steps to building body respect may follow in any order and require a variety of approaches. Among them are the following:

- ■ Enjoy your body!
- ■ Recognize your value and respect your uniqueness.
- ■ Be proud of who you are.
- ■ Remember that your struggles with food or weight or exercise—or anything for that matter—make you no less worthy of respect than others.

Your primary source of transformational power lies in self-acceptance. This doesn't mean that we ignore the damage done by appearance and gender stereotypes or stop trying to change them. But the better you feel about yourself, the less you will measure yourself against external images and expectations, and the less they can trigger insecurity or a drive for a different body or personality. The marketplace would be powerless at promoting self-hatred if we didn't buy into it (and enforce it against one another). The less you judge yourself, the easier it is to step back, think critically, and gain clarity about the links between outside factors and personal troubles. These fresh, politicized perspectives make us more able to act effectively and collectively, strengthening our sense of agency and community.

> The less you judge yourself, the easier it is to
> step back, think critically, and gain clarity about
> the links between outside factors and personal
> troubles.

Caring for yourself doesn't mean that you luxuriate in your perfection all the time. It can be messy and painful. You will have hard days, maybe even hard years. Things happen. Have compassion for yourself. Stick by yourself, especially when things aren't working out as you'd like. Hold on to both self-love and disappointment at the same time. Can you hope to do things differently next time without that having to mean there is something wrong with you now? You deserve that kind of unconditional love from and for yourself.

Here's Looking at You

Are we telling you not to care about your appearance? No! Your appearance is an aspect of who you are, but just one of many traits. *How* you control how you look—whether you dress up or dress down, wear makeup or shave—matters less to your sense of self than your intent. Beauty or grooming rituals can be fun and embolden us. In fact, not caring how we present ourselves to the world can indicate that we're really struggling with life at the moment. But if you're performing the ritual because you think something is wrong with you, or you're nervous about expressing difference, then you're feeling social pressure at work. Taking interest in expressing your identity is different from not being able to go out in the morning without "putting your face on." When you restrict your dressing to vertical stripes to hide your curves, beauty myths are taking their toll in shaming you. But when you dress to celebrate your individuality and other characteristics, the same act can instill confidence.

Beauty or grooming rituals can be fun and embolden us. [. . .] But if you're performing the ritual because you think something is wrong with you, then you're feeling social pressure at work.

What matters is that you define your own standards for what matters and how you present yourself to the world. Trying to fit ourselves into a narrow (literally "narrow!") range of role models can certainly be a pragmatic choice—but it can simultaneously be futile and depressing and shores up the status quo. Instead, name and own your uniqueness, and seek affirmation for it only from others who can see it. Your special combination of attributes builds your life. You are worthy of respect just the way you are.

Not Conforming to Everyone Else

It can be hard to accept your body and build a coherent sense of identity when you are bombarded with messages that you need to change, so remember to show yourself compassion. The more you differ—and *permit yourself* to differ—from the social ideal, the more alone you may feel, at least at first. Conforming to media-imposed beauty standards and socially imposed gender norms is a path of least resistance and may seem easier than challenging them. But is it really easier? In the long run, you will more likely find peace in your body and contentment by throwing over those outwardly determined values and setting up your own yardsticks for attractiveness and value.

To do this, you will need social support and a place to talk about your feelings. In a chicken-and-egg way, you may find that cultivating your internal resources and recognizing your own value makes it easier to build empowering relationships. And any supportive friendships you nurture, intentional communities you join and create, and professional input you seek out can do wonders.

Are you ready to commit to living well the HAES way? Fill out the Body Respect pledge at the back of the book (see page 187).

CHAPTER 10
The Professional Journey

For everyone looking to incorporate the principles of this book and Health at Every Size into clinical or social care, let's return to where we started—contrasting the health impact of personal behaviors like nutrition and lifestyle habits—through the old and new paradigms of weight focus and HAES.

How Health Providers Advise Patients

A Conventional Model

Consider a hypothetical patient, Janet, newly diagnosed with diabetes. Janet feels the stress of balancing full-time work with caring for her two children and disabled father. She has advocated for improved safety conditions at her worksite and worries that her outspokenness threatens her job. Even with overtime, her wages are low. She yearns to take a moment just to sit in the park or treat her children to something special, but lacks the time or money.

Billie, a nurse at her health provider's office, is empathic and experienced, and strives to be patient-centered. She advises Janet to lose weight, eat a more nutritious diet, and engage in more physical activity to manage her diabetes. As if Janet hasn't tried all this! While periodic diets have brought her short-term "success," Janet's always ended up heavier in the long run than before, feeling demoralized and ashamed to boot.

Still, it's not as if Janet doesn't *want* to improve her diet, by adding vegetables, beans, and whole grains, for instance. She does try to "eat right" and is actually meeting many diabetes care recommendations by the time she next meets with Billie. Janet feels less bloated, she notices, and has more energy in the mornings now that she eats breakfast. Her weight is down slightly.

Still, Billie is less than satisfied—for Janet's sake. She points out to Janet that her blood sugar and pressure haven't budged, and she's concerned about the salt content of Janet's diet. When Janet says she's made every change they discussed, Billie seems incredulous. If this were true, she insists, Janet would have dropped more weight and reduced her blood pressure.

Janet is disheartened, and Billie is discouraged. Her years of health care study just aren't worth it, Billie thinks, if even with skilled support and a listening ear, patients like Janet just can't seem to take personal responsibility and follow her recommendations.

Here is why the conventional model is broken. We can look at the supposed facts of the story, but they don't tell the full story. What's really going on in this scenario with Janet and Billie? The conventional model explains weight, blood sugar, and blood pressure as products of diet and exercise. Beholden to this model, Billie believes that Janet's physiological measures would reach the healthy range and she would lose weight predictably, if only she followed medical advice. True, Janet's energy levels, mood, and gut health have improved, but in the conventional model, that counts for little. The traditional paradigm also ignores a significant hidden threat to Janet's goals: her experience of chronic stress.

No matter how she changes her diet or physical habits, the factors that make up Janet's lifeworld—stigma, insecure work, poverty, caring responsibilities—remain unchanged. Healthier eating can improve her sense of well-being and strengthen her against adversity, but it can't remove the stressors she faces. Billie's disappointment and skepticism, in fact, add a new stressor: They give Janet a way to blame herself for not doing better, for failing at weight loss, and even for bringing her diabetes on herself in the first place.

The HAES Model

Now imagine this scenario featuring a Billie who has adopted a Health at Every Size perspective. When Janet makes that first appointment, Billie's sympathetic ear frees Janet to bring up the shame and guilt that surround her dieting history and weight and to share anxieties about embarking on a new round of lifestyle changes. What Janet really wants, she tells Billie, is a diet plan she can *stick to* this time. Billie listens to the challenges Janet faces in altering her lifestyle, so Janet feels heard and respected. *I take your body dissatisfaction and weight concerns seriously*, she assures Janet, before sensitively introducing the idea of a HAES approach.

Together, they make a list of practical suggestions to support Janet in taking care of herself. Eating more regularly is one of them. Another is exploring how her food choices influence her mood and energy levels and how her mood governs what she eats.

This HAES perspective sounds a bit unlikely to Janet—it goes against everything anyone in health care has ever said to her, and now that she has diabetes, which is nothing to toy with, she is even more reluctant to deviate from the conventions she's always known. On the other hand, she knows from experience that the traditional route hasn't been working out very well for her. In fact, she acknowledges, after some discussion, her personal experiences do look astonishingly like the statistical outcomes Billie describes: yo-yoing weight, low mood, and food preoccupation.

By the end of the conversation, Janet may not be a HAES convert, but she feels they have come up with practical steps that can help her, like adding beans and seasonal veggies to meals. And she is intrigued by the HAES imperative of compassionate self-care, even if she's not completely sold on it yet. When Billie explains the links between our histories, life circumstances, and diabetes, it makes sense to Janet. She begins to feel angry at having been hoodwinked into believing her own illness and the high rates of it she sees among her friends and neighbors were all their own fault. She wonders if she's been let down by people she trusted. All this comes with no small measure of relief, as the guilt she's associated with her diagnosis starts to lift.

By her second appointment, Janet's energy levels, mood, and gut health are improved. She is sleeping better and less irritable. More than that, her customary feelings of pre-appointment dread have been replaced by the expectation that she will find herself supported and valued. Members of Janet's church group have noticed her changes and enthusiasm and have invited Billie to give a talk.

In the clinic, when Janet learns her blood pressure has gone up, she suggests it may relate to her struggles at work. She is glad to have the chance to talk about those with Billie. They discuss the pros and cons of blood pressure medication, given that lifestyle changes aren't lowering Janet's blood pressure. But Janet decides to hold off on that in order to give the changes more time.

When she works with patients like Janet (who, unlike some of her patients, at least has a job), Billie can feel overwhelmed at times. She fears that so many social changes are needed for true health improvement in her patient population, and she sometimes feels that she is only a bit player with no impact. Still, she does see a difference already in Janet's emotional resilience, and relishes the chance to speak to the church group. She resolves to check in later with colleagues for support, which may boil down to the useful reminder to keep both the bigger picture and the individual in mind and merely do what we can, when we can. She reminds herself she can't shoulder the burden of the world alone, but that she remains part of a larger social movement that *is* having an impact.

Reframing

While the energy balance equation is expediently simple, HAES has the burden of being somewhat "busy" with all the interconnecting influences on health and lifestyle it recognizes. Those concerned with so-called obesogenic environments may point to a welter of factors, like the food industry, family eating habits, school physical education, climate change, the media, and more, but their fundamental model is the one-dimensional equation, thin = healthy. In other words, it's all about the weight, and mechanistic bodies that are presumed to use calories at a calculable rate with predictable effects. Digestion and metabolism churn on without respect to emotion, personal history, taste, stress, or environmental factors.

HAES philosophy, by contrast, considers health as a multi-faceted endeavor and looks not to fueling a machinelike body but to addressing—and enhancing—people's lived experiences of the world (think respect). In the HAES model, emotions, histories, taste, stress, and so on not only matter, but serve as a basis for a relational understanding of metabolic effect. In other words, *it's not simple*. The model spans and dovetails with the concerns of both self-care and social justice.

In a neat twist, a valuable framework for managing such complexity and translating HAES into action is, well, a sense of coherence. We mentioned this earlier in Chapter 5 and described its key elements. Now we will show how practitioners' holistic approach can serve as a way to introduce new pathways into the therapeutic relationship. A sense of coherence can be a gift to those who seek professional help with feeling out of control around food, and who judge themselves to be dumb, lazy, or weak because of that. It offers a way to make sense of their experiences and render them manageable within a caring relationship. The practitioner can begin by challenging beliefs that equate size with value, or thinness with willpower. She or he can describe why high rates of diabetes or other disease in a client's or patient's community arise from conditions far more complicated than inactivity or an excess of sugar, and offer a compassionate, scientifically valid, alternative viewpoint.

Stories Matter

The old way required practitioners to muscle in on people's lives to impose a lifestyle model of disease addressed by a well-intentioned armory of behavior-change skills and calorie sheets. Its laser focus on the limited parameters of weight, diet, and exercise blinded us to other factors that affect metabolism and health, including the lived realities of inequality. During years of being told "weight loss works," it never occurred to us to question medical authority, and when our patients didn't lose weight, we reckoned we were failing them or they weren't trying hard enough. We doubted their stories and rejected or ridiculed evidence that clouded the picture. Immersed as we were in the delivered wisdom of weight loss as the guiding torch, questions of stigma or otherwise difficult lives just didn't register as relevant or noteworthy. We asked our clients and patients to try harder, to take more "personal responsibility," and we continued to lament the high rates of diabetes and metabolic concerns in populations under threat. We grabbed at straws, for anything that might effect change, like teaching people to cook with more whole grains. In doing so, we abdicated our own personal responsibility to "do no harm." We made decisions that propped up the status quo, reinforced hierarchies of knowledge, and perpetuated shabby science. It can be hard to accept our emotions when we realize what we've been complicit in.

And it comes as a relief to know that there is a new paradigm we can implement straightaway—one that recognizes the importance of relationality, and gives us a different template for the health care relationship. It demands that we think critically about ideas once accepted as fact. In a given week, millions will consult health practitioners for nutrition-sensitive diseases or metabolic syndrome. Think of the impact if they all were treated with dignity and felt heard and understood without blame or shame. If they came away with new ways of thinking about the links among health behaviors, well-being, and disease that affect them and their communities. If their emotional resilience improved, enhancing their self-care behaviors and ability to advocate for themselves. If, when they hit a dip, they were supported with self-care to keep going. If all this were to happen, if HAES became the treatment model, these millions could find new solutions and new allies in the health care community and hope for measurable health improvements that previously proved elusive.

People under threat or in weakened health gain confidence when their stories matter, when they can safely acknowledge their strengths and adversities. They realize problems in their communities that may seem personal, like high blood pressure, might be better addressed by collective solutions, and that their sources may lie not in individual failure but in external demons like racism. And that weight loss—that frustrating, oft-advised quest—may be no kind of solution. What the old paradigm ignores is that, for people beset by the proverbial slings and arrows of hard lives, having someone to talk to about their rage can lead to measurable health improvements and ultimately seed more appropriate responses where conventional dietetics and regular weigh-ins have failed. A shift in nutrition discourse can lead to community cooking clubs that celebrate food cultures and identity, thereby addressing stereotypes to further cohesion. Sharing food knowledge can tackle isolation, build skills, reorient group health narratives, and strengthen relationships, while offering access to nourishing food. This approach is empowering in the true sense of the word: a political process of transformation that starts with self-care. The HAES approach, based on thinking relationally, adds meaning for practitioners as well as the communities they work with.

CONCLUSION

We can sum up in one word what's needed for health improvement: respect. This goes beyond removing fat-phobic images from medical literature or trying to be "kind" or "polite" while persisting within the old, biased weight-focus paradigm. Putting respect into practice means acting to advance social justice. And it means practicing compassionate care and insisting on it for ourselves. So, how can we bring about this effect through our practice, our assumptions and teachings, our conversations, and the decisions we make? And what hidden presumptions must we let go of in order to break down false ideology that stands in the way of health equality and social justice?

Let's recap. Is weight, for example, an essential mediator for health improvement? Conventional thinking assumes so. However, as we've shown, this reading views weight science through a lens of fat phobia and an individualistic lifestyle take on health. In fact, critical analysis of the science indicates that a weight focus not only fails to produce thinner *or* healthier bodies, but even causes damage—damage that extends to increased food and body preoccupation, repeated cycles of weight loss and regain, distraction from more worthy personal health goals and from wider health determinants, reduced self-esteem, potential eating disorders, and general weight stigmatization and discrimination.[1] But when viewed through the lens of body acceptance and a collective, relational take on health, the science suggests a better route to health goals through the very different paradigm of Health at Every Size. The HAES approach does not merely succeed where the fat-focus model fails. HAES succeeds *because* it upends the traditional model, and emphasizes a compassionate, ethical, and *respectful* response to individual and public health concerns.[2]

Digging Deeper

HAES is often called "an alternative to dieting." It is that, but HAES has much deeper goals. To offer a detour from self-blame and a lifestyle focus for health, HAES seeks to loosen the grip that dieting holds on popular imagination. That is why it requires us to step back and consider underlying factors in our worldview, so we don't inadvertently reinforce the very structures we're trying to transform.

Key to this is language. Diet mentality uses a language of duality, where one of a pair must be better or worse than the other—healthy/unhealthy, good/bad, thin/fat, mind/body— with no room for uncertainty or connection or more than two elements. For the source of this kind of binary thinking about the body, look to seventeenth-century philosopher René Descartes, who originated the idea of a mind/body split. While Descartes's views advanced science, they imposed a hierarchy that also can bedevil us. His views of duality led to the idea of human bodies as machines. That framework fosters notions of weight as a simple function of calories in versus calories out, and "good" foods versus "bad" ones, as if our bodies were simple engines running on either regular gas or diesel.

While giving Descartes his due, we must release the idea of rigid dualities before we can stop judging foods, and ourselves, as either good or bad. Given all we now know about the interdependence of our bodies' systems, and the obvious interactions of mind and body, a more holistic view emerges as the only practical prism for health analysis.

Individually speaking, we've already seen how destructive binary thinking can be when applied to eating. Dieters go from feeling morally noble, to feeling punished and out of control, at various stages of the dieting cycle. They must choose between "good" foods and "bad," and apply those same terms to themselves (and others) based not on how they live or act, but on whether they are sticking with their latest diet and, more broadly, are naturally thin or fat. Weight lost equals "success," regardless of the psychic cost, and regain amounts—as we know all too well—equals "failure."

> Dieters go from feeling morally noble, to feeling punished and out of control, at various stages of the dieting cycle.

A World Without Competition?

The judgmental approach becomes a way to think about everything. When we've learned to structure our world through competing categories, we always compare ourselves with other people. Win or lose, there's no common ground. It's become natural to see people as "other" and "us." But what if there was no competition, at least in terms of how we respected ourselves and one another? If our sense of self-worth came from within, that we simply knew we were okay—that we were already clever, attractive, fun, or smart enough—that it was fine to be us? If we can know this, it more easily follows that "my body is not the enemy," leading to the next corollary: that other people's bodies are not "the competition."

What if children learned to respect diversity rather than learning to rank themselves as worth more or less than their friends, based only on size? What if we ditched the diet mentality that attaches so much importance to size and health and fitness, and focused instead on relating to ourselves and one another with understanding and compassion?

HAES in Action: Josie's Experience

Consider "Josie's" path. Josie has a history of dieting, but only recently has begun to understand the logic behind her binge eating. She eats uncontrollably, she realizes, because she has been starving herself every day. That's called survival! Once she allows herself to eat lunch regularly, she begins to feel more in control, and her "I'm home" binges dwindle. She learns to tune in to her emotions and stop judging them as good or bad. Simply noticing what's going on for her enables her to take a step back, and she finds this gives her more clarity. Learning to distinguish her emotional needs from actual biological hunger gives her the control around food that proved so elusive in all the years she worked so hard for it by depriving herself. Now, she gets out of her head more when she eats; rather than worrying about calories, fiber, and portions as she used to, she asks herself which taste, texture, or experience she'd like just now, how hungry she is, and how hungry she wants to be after eating. She feels satisfied after the meal and more in control. As Josie gingerly let go of rigid rules in her food choices, other influences like culture, habit, cost, convenience, packaging, occasion, and so on jostled their way in. She realizes that a healthy relationship with food comes from the totality of the experience, and that reducing a meal to its nutrient profile posed a problem, not a solution. Rather than dreading a workout as a duty to be ticked off at the end of the day, she looks forward to a move-to-music class she really enjoys.

If only she'd been taught how to be kind to herself by the first dietitian she saw all those years ago. Imagine—after waiting all these years to lose weight before trying out the adult education center, last week Josie ended up going without even knowing what weight she was!

What Josie derives from her new, connected way of being in the world is a sense of agency. She had tried so hard for years to "take responsibility" for her health, but ended up failing. The irony is, now that she has let go of the rules she put in place to help her, she is much more able to give her body what it needs. Given what she now knows about social factors and health, she can also see how misleading the focus on personal responsibility is in the first place.

As she lightens up on food rules and begins to think from new perspectives, Josie also finds herself better able to understand others' points of view. Seeing size stigma on TV really gets her goat now, whereas before she felt embarrassed for those being insulted and, even more strongly, ashamed of herself. If she happened to be dieting, she felt smug relief, knowing *she* was "doing something about it." Now, she recognizes how unjust it is to judge others on the basis of what they weigh, and can better resist such harsh judgments against herself. They're still hard to hear, of course, but she is learning ways to speak kindly to herself and will more often turn to others for support.

It is not a simple switch for anyone, including Josie, to look in the mirror and love what they see, and it doesn't even mean managing to like your body 24/7. There are times, as when she takes a seat on a crowded bus, when it's difficult to stay upbeat, because being thin is still so much less demanding than being fat. But at the least, when we go easier on ourselves, it cuts by one (and a very important one) the number of people having a go at us. For Josie, practicing self-care through self-talk and eating to nourish herself adds to her emotional reserves and strengthens her for the challenges and joys of each day. Every week, she's gaining new skills for looking after herself. She notices that even though she's doing more, meeting more people, she has so much more energy and zest. It occurs to her that she no longer avoids social situations where there's food, as it's just not an issue anymore.

Josie and so many of us have spent lifetimes trying to live from the neck up. What we fail to see, while mired in the old paradigm, is the high cost of living this way. Once we take the risk, like Josie, of listening to and valuing our appetites, emotions, and needs—in other words, coming home to our bodies—we enjoy a new sense of clarity. Where once we relied only on intellectual knowledge (or spoken advice), HAES enables us to plot our course with the addition of "embodied" knowledge.

Josie may have come to HAES to lose the weight. But once she embraced HAES, the whole unfolding process has done so much more: She has lost the *burden* of her weight. Josie has suddenly found she feels alive, has clarity, and has also gotten her body back.

[She] may have come to HAES to lose the weight. But once she embraced HAES, the whole un-folding process has done so much more: She has lost the *burden* of her weight.

A Healthy Skepticism

If we're fat, what's new is coming to grips—be that gently or angrily—with what our identity and experience mean to us. Instead of suppressing our fears about fitting in, we embrace intellectual, political, and emotional ambivalence about the context we're asked to fit into. Rather than berating ourselves for being different, we recognize sizeism for what it is and relish the strength we've drawn on to survive it. We seek out role models in size acceptance and fat activism, look for positive depictions in art and media, and draw strength from commonalities with other marginalized groups. Yes, the world can be a harsh place, but we also know it is possible to celebrate and appreciate our bodies and lives. If we are thin (or thinner than others), we learn to reject our fear of fat and stop judging others based on shape. This frees us for a less loaded relationship with food and our bodies, and greater compassion for ourselves and others. We are responsible for addressing the "unearned advantage" we get in the world due to sizeism, and seek to use our thin privilege to make this a more just and compassionate world.

These new perspectives often make people more interested in science than ever, but, rather than swallow every pronouncement as fact, they begin applying analysis and a commonsensical pinch of salt. Skepticism may at first feel unmerited or even disrespectful, especially if we've no formal scientific training. But questioning things from our own perspective can ultimately help us think more critically, test what's true for us, and allow marginalized views to enter the frame. After all, experience with HAES, and the wider perceptions it can lead to, teaches us that truth doesn't always lie in what "most people believe," or what an "expert" says. Questioning, or critical thinking, helps us find collective explanations and solutions to what we once construed as personal problems. It retrains us to look for links between phenomena, and so brings in context. Putting things in context moves us away from reductionist thinking and can help us make sense of what's really going on—that is, it brings a sense of coherence. What we're talking about, in the old parlance, is valuing our own knowledge as a step in the process of consciousness raising.

There's a payoff in more ways than one. By learning to trust ourselves, and our own conclusions about the world, we can be more emotionally present, which strengthens some relationships and lets us walk away from others that no longer feel mutual or supportive. Learning to stand our ground in relationships can in fact lead to a greater intimacy, as well as to just having more fun.

Compassion and Community

Whether our goal is personal health improvement, supporting others as health care practitioners, or effecting structural change as community leaders, the most powerful step on this journey must take place internally. We start by showing compassion to ourselves. Practicing compassion and acceptance helps us build the resilience we need to sustain our ethical integrity in an unjust world. It opens us to a nonjudgmental way of thinking that moves us away from stereotypes and toward greater understanding. It opens our eyes to the personal impact of the social structure and the advantages and disadvantages that social inequality confers. If we are thin or in some other group privileged by bias, we can begin to recognize our unearned advantages. Enhanced compassion provokes us to ask questions that fall outside traditional parameters, and we open ourselves to the implications of what we learn in response. It gives us the courage to act and the capacity to go easy on ourselves when we can't. Along this route, we find that other people can support us in our journey to acceptance and change.

Sounds far-fetched? Check out the huge online community around HAES, size acceptance, Critical Dietetics, and fat activism. Cast your net wider, and you'll find other angles, including critical public health.

The most powerful step on this journey must take place internally. We start by showing compassion to ourselves.

When we are no longer destined to follow the same-old, same-old canard of *eat less, exercise more*, what will we say instead?

"Go gently."

Body Respect Pledge

Today, I will try to feed myself when I am hungry and honor my body's signals of fullness.

Today, I will try to be attentive to how my body feels and to choose foods that make me feel good.

Today, I will try to look kindly at my body and to treat it with love and respect.

Today, I will try to practice more mindfulness.

Today, I will try to challenge stereotype, size bias, and thin privilege.

Today, I will show more compassion toward myself and others.

Signed: _____

SOURCE NOTES

Introduction

1. Jacqui Gingras and Charlotte Cooper, "Down the Rabbit Hole: A Critique of the ® in HAES®," *Journal of Critical Dietetics* 1, no. 3 (2012): 2–5.
2. Charlotte Cooper, "A Queer and Trans Fat Activist Timeline: Queering Fat Activist Nationality and Cultural Imperialism," *Fat Studies: An Interdisciplinary Journal of Body Weight and Society* 1, no. 1 (2012): 61.

SECTION 1: DECONSTRUCTING WEIGHT

Chapter 1—Facts and Fiction about Fatness

1. Charlotte Biltekoff, "The Terror Within: Obesity in Post 9/11 U.S. Life," *American Studies* 48, no. 3 (2007): 29–48.
2. "Surgeon General to Cops: Put Down the Donuts," CNN.com, March 2, 2003, www.cnn.com/2003/HEALTH/02/28/obesity .police/index.html.
3. Linda Bacon, *Health at Every Size: The Surprising Truth about Your Weight*, 2nd ed. (Dallas: BenBella Books, 2010).
4. K. M. Flegal, B. I. Graubard, D. F. Williamson, and M. H. Gail. "Excess Deaths Associated with Underweight, Overweight, and

Obesity." *Journal of the American Medical Association* 293, no. 15(2005): 1861–67.

5. Amy Erdman Farrell, *Fat Shame: Stigma and the Fat Body in American Culture* (New York: NYU Press, 2011), 13.

6. "Overweight and Obesity: Clearing the Confusion," transcript, Centers for Disease Control and Prevention, last modified June 2, 2005, www.cdc.gov/media/transcripts/t050602.htm.

7. Vaughn W. Barrya et al., "Fitness vs. Fatness on All-Cause Mortality: A Meta-Analysis," *Progress in Cardiovascular Diseases* 56, no. 4 (2014): 382–90, doi: 10.1016/j.pcad.2013.09.002.

8. Ibid.

9. R. M. Puhl, T. Andreyeva, and K. D. Brownell, "Perceptions of Weight Discrimination: Prevalence and Comparison to Race and Gender Discrimination in America," *International Journal of Obesity* 32, no. 6 (2008): 992–1000, doi: 10.1038/ijo.2008.22.

10. P. Muennig et al., "I Think Therefore I Am: Perceived Ideal Weight as a Determinant of Health," *American Journal of Public Health* 96, no. 9 (2008): 1662–68, doi: 10.2105/AJPH.2007.114769.

11. Look AHEAD Research Group and R. R. Wing, "Long Term Effects of a Lifestyle Intervention on Weight and Cardiovascular Risk Factors in Individuals with Type 2 Diabetes: Four Year Results of the Look AHEAD Trial," *Archives of Internal Medicine* 170, no. 17 (2010): 1566–75, doi: 10.1001/archinternmed.2010.334.

12. S. Klein et al., "Absence of an Effect of Liposuction on Insulin Action and Risk Factors for Coronary Heart Disease," *New England Journal of Medicine* 350, no. 25 (2004): 2549–57.

13. "Social Determinants of Health," Centers for Disease Control and Prevention, 2014, www.cdc.gov/socialdeterminants/FAQ html.

14. Michael Marmot and Richard G. Wilkinson, eds., *Social Determinants of Health: The Solid Facts*, 2nd ed. (Copenhagen, Denmark: World Health Organization, 2003).

15. Ibid.

16. Ibid.

17. "Social Determinants of Health," Centers for Disease Control and Prevention.

18. A. R. Tarlov, "Public Policy Frameworks for Improving Population Health," *Annals of the New York Academy of Sciences* 896 (1999): 281–93.

19. Tarlov, "Public Policy Frameworks" quoted in "Social Determinants of Health," Centers for Disease Control and Prevention, 2014. www.cdc.gov/socialdeterminants/FAQ.html.

20. E. G. Brunner, T. Chandola, and M. G. Marmot, "Prospective Effect of Job Strain on General and Central Obesity in the White-hall II Study," *American Journal of Epidemiology* 165, no. 7 (2007): 828–37.

21. Michael G. Marmot, "Status Syndrome: A Challenge to Medicine," *Journal of the American Medical Association* 295, no. 11 (2006): 1304–7.

22. Cynthia L. Ogden et al., *Prevalence of Obesity in the United States, 2009–2010* (NCHS Data Brief no. 82) (Hyattsville, MD: U.S. Department of Health & Human Services, Centers for Disease Control and Statistics, National Center for Health Statistics, January 2012).

23. Writing Group for the SEARCH for Diabetes in Youth Study Group et al., "Incidence of Diabetes in Youth in the United States," *Journal of the American Medical Association* 297, no. 24 (2007): 2716–24.

24. J. Robison, "Helping with Harming: Kids, Eating, Weight & Health," *Absolute Advantage* 7 (2007): 1–15.

25. M. Yeargin-Allsopp et al., "Prevalence of Autism in a US Metropolitan Area," *Journal of the American Medical Association* 289, no. 1 (2003): 49–55.

26. E. Odding, M. E. Roebroeck, and H. J. Stam, "The Epidemiology of Cerebral Palsy: Incidence, Impairments and Risk Factors," *Disability and Rehabilitation* 28, no. 4 (2006): 183–91.

27. March of Dimes, "Birth Defects: Down Syndrome," last modified July 2009, www.marchofdimes.com/baby/down-syndrome.aspx.

28. T. J. Mathews, F. Menacker, and M. F. MacDorman, "Infant Mortality Statistics from the 2001 Period Linked Birth/Infant Death Data Set," *National Vital Statistics Reports* 52, no. 2 (2003, September 15): 1–28.

29. L. Ries et al., eds., *SEER Cancer Statistics Review, 1973–1999* (Bethesda, MD: National Cancer Institute, 2002).

30. Writing Group et al., "Incidence of Diabetes."

31. K. R. Merikangas et al., "Lifetime Prevalence of Mental Disorders in U.S. Adolescents: Results from the National Comorbidity Survey Replication—Adolescent Supplement (NCS-A)," *Journal of the American Academy of Child and Adolescent Psychiatry* 49, no. 10 (2010): 980–9.

32. M. K. Serdula et al., "Do Obese Children Become Obese Adults? A Review of the Literature," *Preventive Medicine* 22, no. 2 (1993): 167–77.

33. Charlotte M. Wright et al., "Implications of Childhood Obesity for Adult Health: Findings from Thousand Families Cohort Study," *BMJ* 323 (2001): 1280–84.

34. F. E. Braddon et al., "Onset of Obesity in a 36 Year Birth Cohort Study," *BMJ (Clinical Research Edition)* 293 (1986): 299–303.

35. J. Robison, "Helping with Harming."

36. A. M. Rocandio, L. Ansotegui, and M. Arroyo, "Comparison of Dietary Intake among Overweight and Non-overweight Schoolchildren," *International Journal of Obesity and Related Metabolic Disorders* 25, no. 11 (2001): 1651–55.

37. Ihuoma U. Eneli, Peggy A. Crum, and Tracy L. Tylka, "The Trust Model: A Different Feeding Paradigm for Managing Childhood Obesity," *Obesity* 16, no. 10 (2008): 2197–204.

38. E. M. Satter, "Internal Regulation and the Evolution of Normal Growth as the Basis for Prevention of Obesity in Children," *Journal of the American Dietetic Association* 96, no. 9 (1996): 860–64.

Chapter 2—Weight Regulation

1. K. R. Westerterp, "Diet Induced Thermogenesis," *Nutrition and Metabolism* (London) 1, no. 1 (2004): 5.
2. K. J. Acheson et al., "Nutritional Influences on Lipogenesis and Thermogenesis after a Carbohydrate Meal," *American Journal of Physiology* 246, no. 1, pt. 1 (1984): E62–E70.
3. C. Bouchard et al., "Linkage between Markers in the Vicinity of the Uncoupling Protein 2 Gene and Resting Metabolic Rate in Humans," *Human Molecular Genetics* 6, no. 11 (1997): 1887–89.
4. J. C. Clapham et al., "Mice Overexpressing Human Uncoupling Protein-3 in Skeletal Muscle Are Hyperphagic and Lean," *Nature* 406, no. 6794 (2000): 415–18.
5. Jeffrey M. Friedman, "Modern Science versus the Stigma of Obesity," *Nature Medicine* 10 (2004): 563–69.

Chapter 3—Weight-Loss Realities

1. M. W. Schwartz, "Brain Pathways Controlling Food Intake and Body Weight," *Experimental Biology and Medicine* 226 (2001): 978–81.
2. Jeffrey M. Friedman, "Modern Science versus the Stigma of Obesity," *Nature Medicine* 10 (2004): 563–69.
3. S. Wooley and O. Wooley, "Should Obesity Be Treated at All?" in *Eating and Its Disorders*, eds. A. J. Stunkard and E. J. Stellar (New York: Raven; 1984), 185–92.
4. J. Garrow, *Energy Balance and Obesity in Man* (New York: Elsevier, 1974).
5. L. E. Braitman, E. V. Adlin, and J. L. Stanton Jr., "Obesity and Caloric Intake: The National Health and Nutrition Examination Survey of 1971–1975 (HANES I)," *Journal of Chronic Disease* 38, no. 9 (1985): 727–32.

6. W. S. Yancy, C. C. Wang, and M. L. Maciejewski, "Trends in Energy and Macronutrient Intakes by Weight Status over Four Decades," *Public Health Nutrition* 16 (2013, January): 1–10.

7. Garrow, *Energy Balance and Obesity*.

8. S. C. Wooley, O. W. Wooley, and S. Dyrenforth, "Theoretical, Practical and Social Issues in Behavioral Treatments of Obesity," *Journal of Applied Behavior Analysis* 12, no. 1 (1979): 3–25.

9. C. Bouchard, "Genetics of Obesity: Overview and Research Directions," in *The Genetics of Obesity*, ed. C. Bouchard (Boca Raton, FL: CRC Press, 1994), 223–33.

10. Kristian Tambs et al., "Genetic and Environmental Contributions to the Variance of the Body Mass Index in a Norwegian Sample of First- and Second-Degree Relatives," *American Journal of Human Biology* 3, no. 3 (1991): 257–67.

11. C. Bouchard et al., "Inheritance of the Amount and Distribution of Human Body Fat," *International Journal of Obesity* 12, no. 3 (1988): 205–15.

12. Hermine H. M. Maes, Michael C. Neale, and Lindon J. Eaves, "Genetic and Environmental Factors in Relative Body Weight and Human Adiposity," *Behavior Genetics* 27, no. 4 (1997): 325–51.

13. T. Rice et al., "Familial Clustering of Abdominal Visceral Fat and Total Fat Mass: The Québec Family Study," *Obesity Research* 4, no. 3 (1996): 253–61.

14. A. J. Stunkard et al., "An Adoption Study of Human Obesity," *New England Journal of Medicine* 314, no. 4 (1986): 193–98.

15. D. B. Allison et al., "The Heritability of Body Mass Index among an International Sample of Monozygotic Twins Reared Apart," *International Journal of Obesity* 20, no. 6 (1996): 501–6.

16. Albert J. Stunkard et al., "The Body-Mass Index of Twins Who Have Been Reared Apart," *New England Journal of Medicine* 322 (1990): 1483–87.

17. A. J. Stunkard, T. T. Foch, and Z. Hrubec, "A Twin Study of

Human Obesity," *Journal of the American Medical Association* 256, no. 1 (1986): 51–54.

18. Jeffrey M. Friedman, "Modern Science versus the Stigma of Obesity," *Nature Medicine* 10 (2004): 563–69.

19. P. Williams et al., "Concordant Lipoprotein and Weight Responses to Dietary Fat Change in Identical Twins with Divergent Exercise Levels 1," *American Journal of Clinical Nutrition* 82, no. 1 (2005): 181–87.

20. Stunkard et al., "Body-Mass Index of Twins."

21. Friedman, "Modern Science versus the Stigma of Obesity."

22. Eric Ravussin et al., "Effects of a Traditional Lifestyle on Obesity in Pima Indians," *Diabetes Care* 17 (1994): 1067–74.

23. C. Bouchard et al., "The Response to Long-Term Overfeeding in Identical Twins," *New England Journal of Medicine* 322 (1990): 1477–82.

24. E. T. Poehlman et al., "Heredity and Changes in Body Composition and Adipose Tissue Metabolism after Short-Term Exercise-Training," *European Journal of Applied Physiology* 56, no. 4 (1987): 398–402.

25. C. Bouchard, *The Journal of the Federation of American Societies for Experimental Biology* (1992): 1647 (Abstract).

26. Thomas. A. Wadden et al., "One-Year Weight Losses in the Look AHEAD Study: Factors Associated with Success," *Obesity* (Silver Spring, MD) 17, no. 4 (2009): 713–22.

Section 2: Reconstructing Respect

Chapter 4—Health at Every Size: Personally Speaking

1. Jeffrey M. Friedman, "Modern Science versus the Stigma of Obesity," *Nature Medicine* 10 (2004): 563–69.

2. Linda Bacon et al., "Evaluating a 'Non-diet' Wellness Intervention

for Improvement of Metabolic Fitness, Psychological Well-Being and Eating and Activity Behaviors," *International Journal of Obesity* 26, no. 6 (2002): 854–65.

3. Linda Bacon, "Tales of Mice and Leptin: False Promises and New Hope in Weight Control," *Healthy Weight Journal* 17, no. 2 (2003): 24–27.

4. Linda Bacon et al., "Size Acceptance and Intuitive Eating Improve Health for Obese, Female Chronic Dieters," *Journal of the American Dietetic Association* 105, no. 6 (2005): 929–36.

5. Ibid.

Chapter 5—Health at Every Size: The Body Politic

1. S. Jay Olshansky et al., "A Potential Decline in Life Expectancy in the United States in the 21st Century," *New England Journal of Medicine* 352 (2005): 1138–45.

2. Donna L. Hoyert and Jiaquan Xu, "Deaths: Preliminary Data for 2011," *National Vital Statistics Reports* 61, no. 6 (2012, October 10): 1–52.

3. Ibid.

4. National Center for Health Statistics, *Health, United States, 2007, with Chartbook on Trends in the Health of Americans* (Hyattsville, MD: U.S. Department of Health & Human Services, Centers for Disease Control and Statistics, National Center for Health Statistics, 2007).

5. Wayne Rosamond et al., "Heart Disease and Stroke Statistics—2008 Update. A Report from the American Heart Association Statistics Committee and Stroke Statistics Subcommittee," *Circulation* 117 (2007): e25–e146.

6. Colin D. Mathers and Dejan Loncar, "Projections of Global Mortality and Burden of Disease from 2002 to 2030," *PLOS Medicine* 3 (2006, November 28): 2011–29, www.plosmedicine.org/article /info%3Adoi%2F10.1371%2Fjournal.pmed.0030442.

7. Social Security Administration, "Period Life Table, 2009," www .ssa.gov/OACT/STATS/table4c6.html.

8. E. J. Brunner et al., "Adrenocortical, Autonomic, and Inflammatory Causes of the Metabolic Syndrome: Nested Case-Control Study," *Circulation* 106, no. 21 (2002): 2659–65.

9. Ibid.

10. P. M. Lantz et al., "Socioeconomic Factors, Health Behaviors, and Mortality: Results from a Nationally Representative Prospective Study of US Adults," *Journal of the American Medical Association* 279, no. 21 (1998): 1703–8.

11. G. Behrens et al., "Healthy Lifestyle Behaviors and Decreased Risk of Mortality in a Large Prospective Study of U.S. Women and Men," *European Journal of Epidemiology* 28, no. 5 (2013): 361–72.

12. Michael G. Marmot, "Status Syndrome: A Challenge to Medicine," *Journal of the American Medical Association* 295, no. 11 (2006): 1304–7.

13. J. G. Logan and D. J. Barksdale, "Allostasis and Allostatic Load: Expanding the Discourse on Stress and Cardiovascular Disease," *Journal of Clinical Nursing* 17, no. 7B (2008): 201–8.

14. D. Kuh et al., "Life Course Epidemiology," *Journal of Epidemiology & Community Health* 57, no. 10 (2003): 778–83.

15. M. P. Kelly et al., "A Conceptual Framework for Public Health: NICE's Emerging Approach," *Public Health* 123, no. 1 (2009): e14–e20.

16. Ibid.

17. D. Skuse, S. Reilly, and D. Wolke, "Psychosocial Adversity and Growth During Infancy," *European Journal of Clinical Nutrition* 48, suppl. 1 (1994): S113–S130.

18. QRISK® 2-2013 Risk Calculator at www.qrisk.org.

19. The Scottish Government, "Scottish Index of Multiple Deprivation," last modified March 11, 2014, www.scotland.gov.uk /Topics/Statistics/SIMD.

20. B. Lindström and M. Eriksson, "Contextualizing Salutogenesis

and Antonovsky in Public Health Development," *Health Promotion International* 21, no. 3 (2006): 238–44.

21. Julianne Holt-Lunstad, Timothy B. Smith, and J. Bradley Layton, "Social Relationships and Mortality Risk: A Meta-analytic Review," *PLOS Medicine* 7 (2010, July 27), www.plosmedicine.org.

22. The *PLOS Medicine* Editors, "Social Relationships Are Key to Health, and to Health Policy," *PLOS Med* 7, no. 8 (2010): e1000334, doi:10.1371/journal.pmed.1000334.

23. J. Ludwig et al., "Neighborhoods, Obesity, and Diabetes—A Randomized Social Experiment," *New England Journal of Medicine* 365, no. 16 (2011): 1509–19, doi: 10.1056/NEJMsa1103216.

24. Jane Derges et al., "'Well London' and the Benefits of Participation: Results of a Qualitative Study Nested in a Cluster Randomised Trial," *BMJ Open* 4, no. 4 (2014): e003596, doi:10.1136/bmjopen-2013-003596.

Section 3: Self-Care

Chapter 6—Eating Well

1. R. G. Kuijer and J. A. Boyce, "Chocolate Cake. Guilt or Celebration? Associations with Healthy Eating Attitudes, Perceived Behavioural Control, Intentions and Weight-Loss," *Appetite* 74 (2014): 48–54.

2. David A. McCarron, "The Dietary Guideline for Sodium: Should We Shake It Up? Yes!" *American Journal of Clinical Nutrition* 71, no. 5 (2000): 1013–19.

3. Leann L. Birch et al., "The Variability of Young Children's Energy Intake," *New England Journal of Medicine* 324 (1991): 232–35.

4. E. M. Satter, "Internal Regulation and the Evolution of Normal Growth as the Basis for Prevention of Obesity in Children," *Journal of the American Dietetic Association* 96, no. 9 (1996): 860–4.

Chapter 7—Enthused to Move

1. Linda Bacon et al., "Size Acceptance and Intuitive Eating Improve Health for Obese, Female Chronic Dieters," *Journal of the American Dietetic Association* 105, no. 6 (2005): 929–36.

Conclusion

1. Linda Bacon and Lucy Aphramor, "Weight Science: Evaluating the Evidence for a Paradigm Shift," *Nutrition Journal* 10 (2011): 9.
2. Ibid.

INDEX

ABOUT THE AUTHORS

Linda Bacon, PhD, and Lucy Aphramor, PhD, RD, are widely recognized for their expertise in translating Health at Every Size® (HAES) theory into practice on both sides of the Atlantic. They are coauthors of the groundbreaking "Weight Science: Evaluating the Evidence for a Paradigm Shift," a peer-reviewed study that challenges conventional thinking and has upended complacency in weight-loss research. Their training workshops, considered "transformative" and "life-changing" by participants, are helping many professionals develop confidence delivering the HAES message, and their motivational talks are inspiring lay and professional audiences to look at weight, health, and bodies through different eyes.

Linda, an internationally recognized interpreter of HAES science, is a professor in the Health Education Department at City College of San Francisco; serves as an associate nutritionist at the University of California, Davis; and holds graduate degrees in physiology, psychology, and exercise metabolism, with a specialty in nutrition. Linda has conducted federally funded studies on diet and health, and is well published in top scientific journals. She is a sought-after public speaker and appears regularly in international print, and on radio, TV, and

Internet outlets. Linda has conducted federally funded studies on diet and health, is well published in top scientific journals, and is the author of the paradigm-shifting *Health at Every Size: The Surprising Truth about Your Weight.*

Lucy, a dietitian and Visiting Research Fellow at Glyndŵr University in Wales, pioneered HAES in the U.K.'s National Health Service. She developed the creative HAES course "Well Now," now available internationally through licensed facilitators, which shows how to practically teach the personal-political-physiological rubric in community health groups. Lucy is widely published, often collaboratively, in health and social science journals, Fat Studies, and critical weight science books. Her work is characterized by a strong commitment to ethics, including naming and addressing the embodied impact of poverty, trauma, and oppression. She speaks regularly to lay, practitioner, and academic audiences.

Passionate, charismatic, and informative, Linda and Lucy bring scientific authority, clinical expertise, personal experience, and simple compassion to their writing, speaking, and teaching on HAES, weight, health, and social justice.